BAMBOO LEAVES

BY

BRIAN TAYLOR

www.lulu.com

Other publications:

Blindness-Kindness
Worm's Eye View
Going Out there is No Other
Coming Back there is No Trace
Basic Buddhism for a World in Trouble
Blondin and Other Poems
Toi et Moi
Oxford Poems

ISBN 978-1-4092-7625-8

Copyright © 2007 Brian F Taylor

For Freddie who might

INTRODUCTION

Early morning street markets. Mists and half darkness. Portable charcoal stoves flare up and mix their smoke with the smells of pork and fish and sewers. Monks carry begging bowls. Blind musicians have donation boxes to lighten their darkness. Cobblers display their boxes of tools. A man with a treadle sewing machine mends anybody's anything. Stalls are piled high with fish, twenty different kinds of fruit, sticky rice, steaming pots of vegetables. Brooms, clothing, lottery tickets, buddha amulets, shoes, bicycles, motorbikes. Buyers, sellers, beggars. Policemen with revolvers at the hip. Dogs, cockroaches, rats. A fortuneteller has spread out a brightly patterned cotton cloth, her cards neatly laid out. Waiting.

A multilayered world. Disabled beggars with plastic cups, black Ferraris and a snow-white Bugatti Veyron; a swimming pool which is filled with ice to celebrate every New Year's Day; westernised nose jobs and eyelid surgery; massage parlours; gold and silversmiths, emeralds, rubies and star sapphires; ladyboys and budget sex changes; ghosts and Spirit Doctors; mediums offering lunch to the spirits that possess them; body snatchers lurking below motorway bridges; menus with one-day dry pig and son-in-law's testicles.

Everywhere, temples thunder out their disenchanting message that all this teeming world, its glamour, excitement and misery, is impermanent, not-self and suffering.

Here, the lives of men and women are rounded not with a sleep but a silence. There is a bareness to their lives, an ordinariness, which is itself extraordinary.

There is poetry (and humour) in everyday happenings even without poetic language. They reveal dimensions and levels of being of which we are usually unaware. Because we don't believe in them.

We believe what we see. But we tend to see what we believe. We therefore filter out much of our world, both its richness and its horror.

There is poetry in Thai, Pali and Chinese names, in their meanings and the music of their sounds. I have tried to transliterate the originals and provide translations.

Parents often consult monks or Brahmins about the astrological suitability of names or as to whether they are auspicious. Certainly some names seem very apt. Maybe their bearers grow to fit them. However, everything is complicated by the fact that Thais universally have nicknames. These they use for everything except filling in forms. These are poetic too. (The nicknames, not the forms.)

Originally, poetry everywhere was chanted or sung. If it is not, at the very least it should be read aloud. The intellectual eye, skimming the text in search of a quick-fix meaning, moves too fast to catch the sound and rhythm. It will therefore miss layers of meaning too. How much of the landscape can you see from an express train?

Nowadays a man decides for himself that what he writes is poetry. His readers often disagree. Come to think of it, wasn't it the same in John Keats' time?

The people and incidents are recorded as they were. The perspective and tone varies.

A few poems are included here, which originally appeared elsewhere.

BAMBOO LEAVES

From the sun's fierce heat,
the bamboo grove offers much relief.
Each leaf is uniquely made
and all are quite the same.
The whole provides a living shade;
why give each leaf
its individual name?

The mind is such
a lonely, fragile thing,
so easily afraid
of what it can't believe in.
Yet every time we make-believe,
belief is truly made.

POEMS

Poems are diamonds,
everywhere
embedded in living rock.

You see them
you dig them out
you polish them.

(Sometimes you don't see them.)

Polish them too much,
they break into fragments,
blow away,
a handful of dust.

(Each mote of which is a diamond.)

HOW IT WAS THEN

In Vientiane, Opium Dens are legal,
are controlled by the army.
In Nong Douang Market,
marihuana is sold in bunches
with other dried culinary herbs.

When the nightclub hostesses
want to attract customers,
they take off *all* their clothes
and seem about seventeen.

The Associated Press correspondent
buzzes like a honeybee,
politician to politician,
general to general,
gathering news and views
on political backbiting
and a war that, it appears,
they have been fighting
for almost twenty years;
ever since the end of World War Two.

Today, it is a peaceful, yesterday's town,
French colonial houses, gardens overgrown,
café culture, tree-lined avenues.
Our colonial-style hotel is cheap.
The French food is good.

The Mekhong River flows
between Laos and Thailand.
It starts with Himalayan snows,
filling up with monsoon rains as it goes.
This year it has accumulated the most floodwater
since the 1940s. It has risen twelve metres
and is now level with its bank at the riverside hotel.
Another inch and the river will defeat us
and the whole of Vientiane will flood as well.
Soldiers have been taken from the battlefield
to pile up sandbags along the riverbank.
The river is a torrent carrying houses and trees
and the loss of life's necessities.

The American Embassy has built a wall
in front of its gates where a large marine waits
to make sure the visitors who climb over it don't fall.

Floodwater has reached the airport runway;
there are now no more commercial flights.
Trains have stopped running from Nongkai.
Vans tour the streets with flashing lights
telling us to remain calm, please
(warning of possible outbreaks of disease).
Riverside houses have been abandoned.
The generator, on which the city
depends for water and electricity,
will go out of action the minute
floodwater gets in it.

We ask the American Embassy,
Can they help? No, they can't.

Life has come to a standstill.
We are on an island in the middle
of the Mekhong river surrounded,
not only by a flood we did not choose,
but also by the swirling torrents of a war
which no one will win and everyone will lose.

The next afternoon there is a phone call for Joe.
If we can pack in two minutes and be ready to go,
there's a chance of the help we were asking for.
We pack, we rush out through the hotel door.
The American Consul is waiting
in a Mercedes with its engine running.
In the car, he turns to me with Southern courtesy,
"It was for four American citizens I was sent.
 If you want to be rescued by the US Military,
 you'd better lose that British accent."

A high-speed race through every backway
to where a helicopter stands its ground,
looking like an alien bird of prey,
in the middle of a temple compound.
We run, instinctively ducking
the downrushing wind of its blades,
and are bundled inside safely.
They don't close the doors
and it's water, water, as far as the eye can see.

At the airport, an Army C31,
its engines roaring.
Another run
and we are on board.

We hit water on the runway
with a splash which tests
our safety belts,
bounces us into the air
and we are up and on our way
to Bangkok.

The girls go into the cockpit
with the captain.
Joe and I stay with the crew;
tired, unseeing men,
withdrawn into their heads.

After half an hour, the captain comes to brief us:
The plane's visit to Vientiane was unofficial.
It had no business to be in Laos at all.
So, when anybody asks you, Thai or American,
you just say you got on the plane in Udon.
But, I say, the plane isn't going anywhere near Udon!
Right, he says. And that's where you got on.

I think. I understand.
Laos is a neutral zone guaranteed by a Geneva Agreement.
We are in some kind of gunrunner,
used to drop arms and men into Vietnam.

We arrive in Bangkok
as illegal immigrants.
Stamps in our passports
show we left Thailand.
There is nothing to show
we came back in.

We report to the U.S. Military Reception
and tell our official story:
how we hired a boat to cross
the river into Thailand;
how, because of the chaos,
we were unable to report to Immigration;
how we hired a Land Rover and
made our way overland
(though railway lines and roads were flooded!)
to Udon where we hitched a lift on a plane.

The U.S. Military listens with a disbelieving look.
Not only is it against every regulation in the book
for civilians to fly in military aircraft anyway,

BUT no planes came in from Udon today!
Are we sure? We are sure. We're here!
Can you remember the aircraft number?
We couldn't see one from inside.
He is afraid of being compromised
and sends us and our story to the Thais.

We lay out our bags for inspection.
"Where are you from?"
Obediently, we say, "Udon."
"That's Domestic. You don't need Immigration."
The PCVs' bags contain bunches of marihuana,
bought from the stall in Nong Douang.
They are relieved their luggage escapes investigation.

That should have been the end of it.

Next day,
the two Peace Corps Girls have to go.
They are due to fly back to the States
and we go to the airport to see them on their way.
Oh, say the Thais, your passports show
you have already left the country
and didn't come back again.
We tell them we *did*. Last night.
On a US military airplane.
The Thais say they have no record there
of a military aircraft coming in last night from anywhere.

The girls' plane is due to leave in thirty minutes.

We go back to the U.S. Military
and tell them the truth with every detail.
The USM listens in surprise,
"Say, you guys, have you ever spent a night in a Thai gaol?"
We repeat it really happened just as we say,
that it's really their fault anyway,
that the plane is leaving in fifteen minutes,
that if the girls are not in it,
their visas will expire and they will be illegal.
They're illegal as hell anyway, says the USM.
But he writes a note for them
which confirms that the truth really happened;
they entered the country in a military plane
and are therefore entitled to leave it again.
We take the note to the Thais.

They are the same Thais as yesterday's Thais.
We put the Note of Truth in their hands
and they cannot believe their eyes.
The Chief Immigration Officer understands.
He says, with oriental courtesy,
"I don't believe you or the U.S. Military!"
However he sees
the girls have Official Passports of PCVs,
are somehow involved with the USM,
and it's not his job to stir up trouble with *them.*
So he accepts the note and lets them through the gate
and they make it to the plane
just in time not to be too late.

HOW IT ALSO WAS

I have no stamp in my passport either.
I shall have difficulty
getting out of a country
I have not come into,
and that I'm not so attached to
that I want to die there.

I tell Sutip.
She laughs.
It's a serious situation!
I show her the page where the visa stamp isn't.
She looks at it carefully
and tells me. Seriously.
"You have no visa stamp!"
I am full of admiration.
She has got to the heart of the matter.
In one.

She picks up the phone
and speaks to Somchai's father.
He says he will send a car here.
Ten minutes later a Mercedes arrives.
"Where are we going?" I ask the driver.
"You don't need to go anywhere, Acharn.
 Please give me your passport."

Later that afternoon, he puts it in my hand.
The Entry Visa proves that I *did* re-enter Thailand;
though not on the day I thought I had.
I arrived, it seems, this morning.

HICKORY DICKORY DOCK

A girl pedals.
A boy with the dream of her shirt in his eye
rides the metal carrier behind,
pressing her feet down with his.

An individualist stays within call.

My shoe cushions a small Chinese forehead
pressing down her eyes
for money.
Another kneels her black passin
into the sand
fingering a tin;
shells she has
collected to sell.
Her child rubs dirt
into the bright stripes of his shirt.

Bird song bird
thing-word-thing
sand-me-sea.
One between two
so that nothing's seen
without involving all the rest;
she, pressing eyelids,
he, with prosperous vest,
leading all the world in
as their relatives.

This remembered and puzzled in sālā-shade,
where I had come
to meet and be alone with my friends,
one between two
(involving infinity) –
when the sun burst into rubbery fire
through the smoked glass of waving branches
at the wind-open western side,
negating aloneness
(or any other kind of activity),
taking the form out of things
and giving glorious light,
swelling the colours on the bananas
until they stained the plate
(destroying a world of physics
with one splash).

MEO

He has dirty feet;
*"Washing is dangerous
  wash much, sicken and die."*
He wears a short black jacket
and floppy black trousers.
A large silver lock hangs round his neck.
She has a blue jacket
and a tightly pleated kilt
of hemp and cotton
with heavily embroidered
and weighted black sashes.
They stand quite still,
look without curiosity
but with open smiles.

Every three or four years their village
moves to a new part of the jungle
and burns the trees and undergrowth.
In the mixture of ash and soil
they grow maize and opium.
They are always on the move.
A hundred years ago they were
driven out of Burma and Yunnan.
They have been driven out of the valleys.
As Hill tribes they are objects of curiosity.
Formerly, the British Government in Burma,
the French in Laos,
the Siamese and Chinese
all bought their opium.
Now their former customers
tell them opium is bad,
they must grow tea or coffee.
They still grow opium
and the Thai police sent to stop them
tax them instead.
Sometimes they pay the tax in opium.
To them it is all the same;
being moved on,
selling their crops,
bribes and taxes
and being poor.

They want to live, they have to pay.
They are objects of curiosity to tourists
and cash crops for missionaries.

DYING RACES OF MANKIND

When the rich see the very poor
they know it is time
to buy their valuables.
Cheaply.

This ancient people
were driven out of Tibet
by the Tibetans,
out of China by the Chinese
and out of Burma
by the Burmese.

Ah Kah people are very poor
and cannot offer much resistance
to economic assistance.
They make exquisite silver jewellery
and headdresses.
Treasure hunters
have been buying them.
Cheaply.

Ah Kah people have bright shining souls.
Christian missionaries
have been buying them.
Cheaply.

Although the missionaries,
have been taught
that moth and rust doth corrupt
and thieves break in and steal,
they courageously bite the moral bullet
and seek treasures on earth as well.

Ah Kah are animists
and see all around them spirits
and the ghosts of their ancestors.
Their villages are small,
their houses bamboo
and on stilts.
They are accustomed
to having to abandon them
and move on.

Outside each village
is a ceremonial swing

on three poles.
Smaller than the Giant Brahmin Swing,
it serves the same purpose;
to gently dislodge the jiva
from the physical manipura
and reawaken the old self-knowledge.

The Headman reawakens
the old tribal-knowledge.
He can recite the names of the ancestors
back to the Beginning.

Carefully carrying
this self-knowledge
and this tribal-knowledge,
carefully preserving
this family identity,
they have wandered on
like Bronze Age tribes.

Like the Israelites,
who recited their ancestral names
in the *Generation of Adam*;
And Adam begat Seth
and Seth begat Enos
and Enos begat Cainan
and Cainan begat Mahalaleel
and Cainan lived eight hundred and forty years
after he begat Mahalaleel...

Like the Ashokhs in Transcaucasia,
reciting the story of Gilgamesh.

All these are Inheritors.

The missionaries are bookworms
and teach the Ah Kah
not to believe in spirits
but to become Christians
and go to heaven after they are dead
(which the missionaries
do not seriously believe in
and to which *they* are unlikely
to be going after they are dead).
The missionaries have already bought
twenty five percent of the Ah Kah souls
in these rolling green hills.

The Spiritual Inheritance of Ah Kah
is bought with running water,
fertilizers and televisions,
radios and motorbikes,
pharmaceutical drugs and jobs
and education for the next generation.

In this village there are two brick buildings,
the priest's house and a Church.
Despite this, the recitations still go on,
as does haruspication
from the entrails of black pigs.

Further down the valley to the east,
that large white building
is where the children eat and sleep;
and are schooled in the virtues
of the neverland
of western industrial society
and its sanitized philosophies.

ULTRA MORES

Among the Meo,
an unmarried mother
is more desirable as a wife
than a virgin.
She has proved her fertility;
her children will be welcome workers
in the family's fields.

JIT AND SUTIP

Jit (Consciousness) is short and round
and laughs heartily
every time he is introduced
to a silence.
He is a lawyer.

Sutip (Happy Angel) is a Thai.
Sutip is a Mon.
Sutip is a Buddhist.
Sutip is a Christian.
Sutip is a teacher.
Sutip is always smiling
from behind tinted spectacles.
She makes the children of the great
her special concern, sailing
her dinghy in the lee of great ships
and displaying
the appropriate flags,
when called upon,
in their correct sequence.

Every year,
Jit and his friend the doctor
fly to Chiengmai
with two prostitutes
for a week.

Sailors learn that even great ships
are vulnerable to tempests
or the erosion of time.
Small boats too face
the vast oceans alone.

NOMADS

Formerly the Lahu were in Yunnan.
Now they have brought their black teeth and black cotton,
their smell of stale sweat and wood smoke
to places like Doi Angkhang.
They build bamboo houses with grass roofs of lalang
and put their ever-smouldering fires
in the middle of the floor where they deter
woodworm and mosquitoes and flare
brightly and noisily for cooking.
The families sleep in pairs around the fire,
feet pointing inwards like spokes of a living wheel
(which is what they are).
Conversation flares up and disappears like firelight
and finally smoulders away into silence.

The bamboo floor starts to shake violently
as there is a sudden flare
of passion in one of the pairs.
This subsides but the contagion spreads
around the circle until everyone is exhausted.

Now the entire building shakes and creaks.
The horses under the house
are rubbing their itchy bodies against the posts.
This frightens the pigs
who run around grunting and snorting
and disturb the dogs
who run out in all directions
and bark until dawn.
The Lahu snore,
the owls hoot.
Just before sunrise
the women pound today's rice
like the rhythmic hammering
of axe-head birds.

At last the cocks crow
and dawn comes up,
not like thunder,
but as a bright cloud of peace
and everyone stays in bed
until the world warms up
and melts the frost.

TALE OF A CHAIR

In Ban Pho,
fifty years ago,
Ah Koh Lai the widow
filled her heart
and saved five thousand baht.
Pressing her hands together in salutation,
she resolved to make a donation
for the benefit of all
to Wat Krathum Uposotha Hall. *

She sent her granddaughter
to Saochingcha where,
by the giant Brahmin Swing,
she bought a giltwood Dhamma Chair.

Wrapped in paper padding;
squeezed into a taxi shaking;
pushed into a bus bumping
(but sideways and at the back).

Fifty miles on tarmac jolting
  to Ta Tua Bridge
  to the shop
  to the jetty
to a boat.

Floated
to the Uposotha Hall
at Wat Krathum.

Rested.
Red lacquer, carved giltwood
and teardrop decoration.
From it, sermons given
on morality
and monks ordained and tested
on the 227 precepts
at the Patimokha Recitation.

* Uposotha: *literally "fasting". In Buddhism,* Uposotha *days are the lunar quarter days set aside for religious observances by both monks and lay people. The* Uposotha Hall *is the Ordination Hall.*

Waited
and outlasted
several constitutional reviews,
three democracies,
five dictators
and approximately seven coups.

Slumbered
until Sunday at three in the morning
when, without warning,
and despite the howling of twenty dogs
and the steel of three padlocks,
burglars clambered
over the wall
and cut their way into the Uposotha Hall.

The Abbot struck the bronze bell.
Each monk came out from his cell
to see what was being done.

Done?
Someone had had a vision;
Buddhism is a profitable religion
in more ways than one.

Stolen:
the Dhamma Chair,
a brass Buddha image
of Luang Por Sothorn,
a vacuum cleaner
(and three damaged padlocks).

Ah Koh Lai's granddaughter
remembered a story the monk had taught her.
The millionaire Sumangala
built a vihāra
for the Buddha
near his palace.
The Brahmin Gamabhojaka
burned it down out of malice.
Sumangala expressed his appreciation
to the unknown arsonist for the conflagration;
"This good man," he reflected,
"has given me
*a wondrous opportunity
to have another vihāra erected
and make more merit!"*

Ah Koh Lai's granddaughter was elated.
"These bad men," she stated,
"have given us, I see,
a wondrous opportunity
to have a new Dhamma Chair donated.

And make more merit!"

CITY OF ANGELS

Shafting sunbeams. misty eddies,
towering, sculpted, shining chedis,
thundering traffic, six lane highways,
swampy, shabby, back-street by-ways,
mangoes, sticky rice, dom yams,
squeezed into the Mother of all Traffic Jams.....

JIEW

Jiew (Tiny) is thirty-one.
He is very strong,
his eye is like a falcon's.
His father is ninety-three,
his mother is dead
(she was his elder sister).
He lives with his father and two brothers.
who are also his nephews.

FULL MOON DAY THIRD LUNAR MONTH

One candle is a light unto itself.
One hundred candles
illuminate a room.
In a room,
one candle is
a light unto itself.

Uposotha Day at Wat Krathum,
seven old ladies and one old man
taking eight precepts for a day
to keep the fires of Hell at bay.
*"I undertake to observe the precept
to refrain from killing living beings.
I undertake to observe the precept
to refrain from taking things not given.
I undertake………"*
An old monk gives a sermon;
*"Articulate Sariputta is blamed.
Ānanda's economy of speech is blamed.
Silent Buddhas are blamed.
Criticising others
burns the heart
wards off wholesome
states of mind."*

A new and lofty concrete sala hall
is being built to house a replica
of a famous Buddha image
in which, they say, Luang Por Sothorn *
floated along the river Bang Pakhong,
against the current, to Chachoengsao
after the sacking of Ayudhaya,
a city of a million souls.

Eleven o'clock,
a bell sounds.
Seven monks follow their abbot

---

* A famous monk who after the fall of Ayudhaya is believed to have rejected Nibbāna and entered a Buddha image for the benefit of others. His cult, widespread in Thailand, is centered on Chachoengsao where it has created an economic boom based on the pilgrim trade there reminiscent of Lourdes and Canterbury in the Middle Ages in Europe. Amulets with his image sell for up to 40,000 baht each.

past a rabble of dogs with mange,
sabbe sangkhārā dukkhā, *
to Jai Hieng's house
on the anniversary
of Jai Hieng's father's death,
sabbe sangkhārā aniccā. **

Off the road,
concrete lintels laid end to end
make a causeway.
To the left a lake
once watered orchards.
The lake remains,
abandoned to monsoon and sun
and the struggle to survive.
The orchards are long since gone
to make way for a ramshackle prison,
an intensive chicken farm;
a hundred yards
of crude, wooden Auschwitz.

Deserted now,
last week's screams
and cackles and sudden death
are an uneasy silence
this hot afternoon.
By government decree,
the chickens have gone.
A thousand and more,
stuffed alive into bags,
thrown into a pit,
a powdering of white lime
on freshly dug earth,
flattened where the tractor has been.

A mass grave
to protect humans
from chicken flu.

In Jai Hieng's house
the monks sit
on coloured rattan mats,
along adjacent walls.

   * *All conditioned things are suffering.*
   ** *All conditioned things are impermanent.*

Fans are trained on them.
A white string links them,
hand to hand,
from abbot's hand
to Ting Lee's urn
in the adjoining room.
They chant
of suffering, impermanence
and insubstantiality.

Two old ladies and one foreigner
listen to the chanting of Pali words
spoken by Buddha himself
over two and a half thousand years ago,
a chant which vibrates
the heart chakra
like a lute string.

No-one else listens.
Food is prepared.
Everyone shouts commands
(and counter-commands).
Plates clatter.
Cutlery rattles.
Monks chant.

They do not need to *listen*
to a language
which, like the liturgies
of medieval Christendom,
is recognised,
revered,
but, by the laity,
not understood.

It is enough that the monks are here,
large and loud,
like a massive, virtual reality
Television Screen.

Afterwards, lunch.
We sit and watch the monks eat,
as in Bangkok
the rich used to pay
to watch the king dine.
Curries, rice, shrimps,
asparagus, carrots, peas,

tofu, sticky rice, dom yam,
lotus seeds, luk deui,
makaam thets, jackfruit, mangoes.

(But no chicken.)

SEE (GRACE)

See is fifty-one.
She works for Boehm
under a roof with one wall,
by a dusty road
that smells of cars,
with no piped water
and no drains.
But there *are* six dogs.

Toyota are erecting a factory
to make car parts.
Boehm has the contract
to feed the builders
three times a day.

All hot day
See stands;
cuts the vegetables
chops the meat
cooks.

She starts at four in the morning,
goes home at eight in the evening.
Some days she gets two hundred baht,
sometimes three,
occasionally four.
(But she doesn't have to wash the plates).
Her legs are swelling up.

Vinay (Discipline) is her husband.
He is fifty.
When he was a teenager
he worked as a bus boy.
One night, See dreamed
he had an accident
and lost a foot.
The next day the bus turned over
and they amputated his left leg.

BOEHM (BIG)

Boehm is Leader of the District Council.
He helps See cook from four till eight,
then he goes to his office.
He bought the land
on which they cook
with borrowed money
to set up a shrimp farm;
a network of flooded concrete tanks
open to the sky;
with propellers to oxygenate the water
and keep the shrimps alive
until it is a convenient time
for them to die.

The shrimp farm failed.
The concrete tanks are dry and dusty.
Boehm owes money
(and about ten thousand lives).

KWANCHAI (VICTORIOUS SPIRIT)

He has a tanker.
He fills it up where
there is fresh water.
He drives to where
there is no water
and sells it there.

CHINESE NEW YEAR

Chinese New Year
always comes in February.
(Usually.)

This is the last
of the twelve year cycle;
the Year of the Pig.

Processions, dragon dances,
fireworks and smoke,
cymbals and drums.

The Chinese close their shops,
do not sweep their houses
and pay respect
to the Ancestors.
They put a spray
of cream and purple orchids
on car radiators.
They put peacock-eye feathers
in the Spirit House of Chao Ti.

This year
a thin woman
hung up her baby
by its left ankle.
She let it bob and scream
as an entertainment.
A silver coloured bowl
collected offerings.
The string broke.
Someone caught the baby.

Muslims exploded bombs,
killed an army major,
burned Buddhist schools.

Someone stole our telephone wire.
(Copper is making a hundred baht a kilo.)

MARTIAL LAW

Since the military coup
seventy-one schools
have been burned down
in the northeast and the south.

To combat this
the army has announced
it is the responsibility
of headmasters
to prevent this happening.

Headmasters
now sleep
in their schools.

JUSTICE

Every year three hundred
are executed
by lethal injection.
In Klong Prem prison,
Lifers have their chains
permanently welded.
One small room contains
fifty prisoners who pay
one visit to the lavatory
every day.

Yesterday morning,
two Russian girls
sat in deckchairs
to watch the sunrise on Koh Samui.
Someone shot them.
They were first-time tourists.

BURGLARIES

Boonrup (Merit Received)
sells food in the Temple shop.
There have been six burglaries.

At first Boonrup called the police.
They came.
They looked.
That's all they did,
except to ask for "petrol money".

The fact that they asked
doesn't mean
they were giving Boonrup
any choice.

A FORK IN THE ROAD

The footsteps of the ancestors fade.
Grass grows in the old tracks
to be followed by scrub and woodland.
The old destinations are deserted,
their treasures forgotten,
the stones looted for a chicken house or barn.

And the new ways lead on
to factories, hospitals, schools
and the further enslavement of the sons of man.

Worapani (She of the Excellent Skin)
is sixty five.
Her family is well to do.
*"I went to Teachers Training College.
Now I sit with a Judge."*
Did you study Law?
"No."
So why do you do this work?
"For fame and honour."
How?
*"We make famous Thai deserts.
Our family business
is prosperous.
If I am seen with a Judge,
Police and Tax Inspectors will not bother us."*

SUPAPORN AT TWO A.M. *

*"Just because you can't see it
doesn't mean it isn't there.*

*If you can't see it,
it means it certainly is there.*

Waiting."

---

* Supaporn: *wholesome blessing*

NONGLAK (BEAUTIFUL WOMAN)

Nonglak is thirty-nine.
She teaches English thirteen hours a week.
Who do you live with, Nonglak?
"I live with mother."
When Nonglak was a baby,
her aunt said to her mother,
*"I have no children.
 Give me your baby."*
So, Nonglak's mother gave her the baby.
She has always called her aunt "mother".
Now her aunt is dead.

For four years,
the coffin has rested in the house
waiting for cremation.

Who do you live with, Nonglak?
*"I live with mother.
 I live with mother!"*

NOT ENOUGH, PLEASE

I am buying pomelos,
papayas,
mangoes.

The dog barks at him furiously,
threatening.
He turns back and comes towards me.

He puts his face very close to mine,
threatening,
with a kind of hungry hatred.
"Acharn, give me money!"
I look at him. He is angry.
Young, full of energy
and angry.
"Give me money, Acharn!"

I give him a silver baht.
"Not enough!"
He touches his shirt.
"I need a shirt!"
I give him a silver baht.

Five minutes later
at the other end of the market,
his face is again pushed into mine.
*"Give me money!
 Give me money!"*
I look at him.
He touches his shorts.
"I need shorts!"
I have given you already.
He goes away.

UNDER THE DARK OF THE VINE VERANDA

Coral dust blows
off the white beach
onto the slatted table.

Overhead, a trellis
of brown wood and green leaves
and, pushing through, dense clusters
of pink and white
Ladies' Finger Nails,
sweet scented with a trace of lime.

An orchestra of cicadas,
the rustling of a million
tiny silver bells.
A fine sprinkling sound.
Like frost.

A CHINESE GIRL IN THE SEA AT SAMET

She smiles as only the young smile.
What is your name?
"Ah Li."
Where are you from?
"Shanghai."
What is your work?
"I am an accountant."
What is your religion?
"I have none."
She smiles.
*"When we are young
 they teach us,
 Don't believe in God.
 Believe in the Committee."*
She smiles.
"My mother is a Buddhist."
What kind?
*"My mother has a Buddha.
 She burns incense.
 She kneels.
 She asks what she wants."*
She smiles.
*"When I am young,
 I have blood cancer.
 My mother pray to her Buddha.
 I get well!
 Maybe one day
 I am a Buddhist."*
She smiles.

The sun is getting hot.
She turns, dives under the water
and swims towards the raft.

THE TEMPLE OF THE DAWN

Having defeated the Burmese,
King Taksin the Great
camped with his army,
the survivors of Ayudhaya,
at Thonburi.
There he built his capital
around the ancient Temple of the Dawn.
Its giant Phrang, sixty-seven metres high,
is decorated with shining fragments
of Chinese porcelain.

A quarter of a millennium later,
his inheritors proclaim:

Please dress up politely.
Please do not climb the rail.
Please do not dangle any doll.
Do not drop cigarette and waste on floor.

The chedi steps are steeply raked
from the four quarters.
They have worn away.
Until halfway, there is no handrail
to compensate
for unsteady feet.
(Do they wait
for Health and Safety to close them down?)
Just here there is a gate
and from there to the top,
new, strong, beautifully-woven, jute rails
run either side of the steps.
As soon as these were safely in place,
this gate was erected,
locked and decorated
with a sign proclaiming CLOSED.

Forty years ago I used to climb
(without handrails)
to look across the river from the top
and admire The City of Angels.
Today I look at the top of the Temple
from this gate
(and admire pristine, jute handrails).

THE NARAI

A scale model of the Royal Barge,
in the form of a Golden Hangsa Bird,
sacred to Siva.
Teak and black lacquer,
gilt and green glass inlay.
Thirty six foot long and eight foot high
with long thin beak and blue glass eyes,
it stands in this great Hall
of Chinese and Italian marble.
A garland of jasmine
hangs from its beak.
Halfway back, its pavilion
is filled with offerings of candles,
incense and chrysanthemums.

In the Ladies' Toilet,
a tall thin girl, in her late teens
and dark blue uniform,
energetically scrubs the marble floor.
She says to Saisamorn
(Beloved Girl),
"You have a foreign boyfriend?"
"Yes."
"Can you arrange one for me?"
"Oh no! This business is for love,
 not for something like that!"

A QUIET WOMAN IS A PEARL IN AN OYSTER

The latest Military Dictator
is a Moslem with two wives.
Cleverly,
he has discovered
that all the kingdom's problems,
insurgency, corruption, poverty,
Suvarnabhumi Airport,
the unseasonal flooding in the northeast,
are the fault of the elected Prime Minister
whom the general has ousted.
Fortunately.

Happily,
he has the support
of many grateful former generals.

AS A THING IS VIEWED, SO IT APPEARS

The Emerald Buddha
is not made of emerald
but a kind of green
and mutton coloured jadestone.

Nor is it a Buddha,
though seated on a gilded throne
above our heads;
though presented every year
with new robes by the King himself;
though credited with magical powers
of healing and the allocation of wealth;
though without any doubt
the guardian and protector of the Kingdom;
though guarded by soldiers.

It is a carved image
of a seated man,
an icon, an atavistic talisman,
the spoil of wars between Thai and Lao.
It is a footprint,
a thousand years of history.

For the past 700 years,
the spirit of Kru Ba,
an old toothless monk in a brown robe,
has lived in the image.
When asked about his motive,
he replies, "I want to help people."

PUBLIC NOTICE

YOU ARE NOW ENTERING SILOM ROAD
THE POLLUTION LEVEL IS VERY HIGH

The terracotta pavement is lined
with pradhu trees,
the symbol of the Navy,
hung with orchids (wooden bananas).

Outside a shop called *"Modern Optical"*
with its reflecting rows
of à la mode spectacles
is a line of large Chinese fish bowls
in which live (and will die)
three-foot high pudtan trees.

On these pots, sit five of the very poor,
hunching together as penguins do,
to keep the outside out.
One is grey with age,
two play old wooden instruments discordantly,
a girl sings;
the harmony is in the poverty.
Each has a tin labelled *"Donations"*.
No eyes are visible in half open sockets.
For they are blind.

They touch to make a living human chain
so that the fragile world they share
does not disintegrate.
A sharp-eyed woman,
with eyes for all five,
assists (or exploits)
their helplessness.

When the owner of Modern Optical
comes out to speak
and wave his hands,
she leads them away
to the market to find a new pitch.
Each holds onto the one in front
like a medieval European dance
of Dies Irae.

"What were they playing?"
The music of human misery.

LEK (SMALL)

Lek is truly not very big.
She is a good cleaner.
She gets under furniture
and into tight corners.

Yesterday, her daughter Ladawan
(Convolvulus)
was bitten by a snake,
Green Snake Burnt Tail.
Usually, a green snake is not poisonous.
(Burnt Tail makes the difference).

She is in Ban Pho hospital.
Her husband won't go to hospital with her.
His sister says, *"not our business".*
Lek will stay with her tonight.

She says, *"I will remember.*
When they are ill, I will remember!"

PHAK CHEE (CORIANDER)

Phak Chee is a female Doberman
who lives next door
with a very small male
called Ai Kee (Mr. Vicky).
She stands on her toes
and is very handsome.
She is fifteen years old.
Although she has a compound
of one and a quarter acres,
she prefers to come
to our three thousand square yards,
twice a day,
to urinate.

Her owner has spent ten million baht
building a teak house,
in the neoclassical style,
with Bangkok period windows,
right up in the sky
on ten foot high
white concrete posts,
She is the Regional Head of the Inland Revenue.
She is also my cousin.

I am always being told
that, in this world,
one ought to try
to make a difference.
Perhaps I should walk up the drive,
twice a day, and stand
close to my neighbour's posts
and make a difference.

"Coriander"
What a name for a dog!

(PS Mr. Vicky does it too.)

NONG AND LEK

Nong (Young) is fifty four.
Lek (Small) is large.
When they were children
(really young and really small),
they fought all the time.
One day, while they were fighting,
they fell into the canal.

Now, of course,
they are good friends.

SOCIAL PROGRESS ON SILOM ROAD

The pavements with red warning stripes
are here twelve inches high
just as they were in England
when carriages thundered by.

Laudably,
England has moved on.
To help the deserving disabled,
it has lowered its pavements
and introduced ramps,
thus wheelchair access
is enabled.

Commendably,
Bangkok has followed suit
with bigger, better ramps
at either end of every stretch of pavement.

England's young cyclists
welcome social progress with glee.
They compete with wheelchairs
and invalid carriages quite happily.

In Bangkok there are few wheelchairs
and no invalid carriages.
But motorbikes, with special messengers
in smart uniforms astride,
ride the march of progress with gratitude,
accelerating and swaying
in and out of stalls of food, clothing and jewellery,
monks with their begging bowls,
beggars with their plastic cups
(and occasional one baht coins)
and white and blue uniformed students.
So much so, that pedestrians who are abled,
protect their feet from two wheels,
by stepping down
among the chainsaw
drone of samlaws
nudging the kerbs,
grubbing for fares,
in the mother of all traffic jams
which is Silom Road.

STARTING OFF ON THE RIGHT FOOT

Phuket is blessed with the
HAPPY TOOTH DENTAL CLINIC,
which offers Preventative Dentistry
and Pediatric Dentistry.

It seems that by preventing teeth
growing in the first place,
they will save you
a lifetime's dental fees.

Like the Jesuits they believe,
*"Get them young enough
 and you have them for life!"*
(Or in this case you won't have them for life.)

Even the Jesuits
didn't think of providing
a set of false teeth
with their first catechism.

UMA DEVI AT HOME IN SILOM ROAD

Every Monday morning
without warning,
cleaners, uniformed in dark blue,
carrying soapy water, are sent
to scrub the pavement
until it's truly glistening.
(Ken Livingston,
Mayor of London,
where are *you*?
Are you listening?)

A black Toyota Fortuna in dark glasses
turns into a market lane,
where you can buy everything
from caged birds to wedding rings,
fighting fish to sugar cane.
It nudges gently as it passes
everything in its air-conditioned way.

"You weren't here yesterday,"

"No" the stallholder turns to me,
"I go to Massage Doctor.
Have pain in knee.
Last night dream about cobra,
big, black, heavy,
pressing down on back.
Can't move. Can't breathe!
Then see
Uma Devi
standing on back.
'Better already!' she say. 'Never mind!'
Wake up already, feel fine."

"You should go to wai Chao Mère."

"Yes, better go.
Give her best mango."

In Chao Mère Uma Devi's temple,
Uma Devi's shrine room is ample
and amply protected by two Brahmins,
with stylish beards and
devotees kneeling at their feet.

Siva, her husband,
(*"May all devotees adore Him!"*)
has a much smaller shrine nearby;
and only one Brahmin,
with one devotee kneeling at *his* feet.
His Brahmin speaks neither English nor Thai
and is uncomfortable with the heat.

It seems that progressive feminism
has infiltrated the Vedas.
Will the sacred lingam
now
bow
to the yoni on Mount Kailas?

"OH TO BE IN ENGLAND..."

The message from England is clear,
"The prisons are full".

The solution is obvious,
"No more people are to be sent to prison!"

For decisions like this
the Home Secretary is paid
£135,337 per year.

Oh Nelson! Oh Wellington! Oh Mr. Chips.

SANGUAN (THE PRESERVER)

He stands at the top of the steps,
very straight.
He has an aluminium stick,
he is eighty-five,
his hair is stark white.
Today he makes merit
because his niece
has driven him to the Temple
from his big, empty house.

His eyes are everywhere, like a lizard's tongue.
He paces restlessly about the sālā
(that is, he shuffles slowly with his stick).

He has three sons in Bangkok.

He owned the last opium den in Chachoengsao
before the Americans paid Field Marshal Sarit
to make them illegal
and close them all down.

(This inaugurated
an even greater trade
in opium and heroin.
Because it was illegal,
the profits were much greater.
Army trucks transported the drugs
quickly and safely
from the Golden Triangle
to Bangkok.
Because it was controlled by the army,
rivals could be executed.
For illegal drug dealing.)

The monks eat,
the overhead fans hum,
the clock chimes the quarters,
the Sermon is on the Perfections.

A small boy clatters
plastic counters
on the teak floor.

PAI DONG

Medhi (The Philosopher)
has an elder sister.
When she left home,
his mother's heart was gloomy,
smouldering.
Rabieb (The Neat One) played Pai Dong;
sitting around in a circle,
fingering the cards and the money,
hoping for Eeo Chee, the Ace,
(fearing Ai Dong Daeng, the Red Cock).
Once she was away for two months,
eating and sleeping in the House of Cards.

The boy stayed home
with his father,
crying at night
as an eleven year old will.
*"Please don't go, mother.
 Please don't go!"*
He had started a new school.
In the evening he fried an egg.

Even when Rabieb came back,
they sent someone every morning.
"Come, Rabieb. For cards."
They brought her back in the evening.
"See you tomorrow, Rabieb."

One day she felt her bad karma had run out.
"This is my last day", she said.
All the players laughed.
"See you tomorrow! See you tomorrow!"
She never went again.

Rabieb's mother, Prae (Cotton Silk)
(who patrolled her rice fields
with a drawn sword)
had played cards when *she* was old.
But how could she compete
with younger hands and eyes?

Prae had no money,
so Rabieb rowed her boat
along the river,
up the canal, to the lock,

selling morning glory,
pickled cabbage, pumpkin,
bananas, bean curds, mackerel.
"Please don't play cards, mother.
Please don't play cards!"
She made her mother angry.
Because of her mother's anger,
Rabieb, too, had fallen under the power
of the Spirit of Pai Dong.

THE HEART OF DARKNESS

The explorer draws his map
and plunges into space.
Why should he stumble on
at every fresh mishap
and draw back in blank surprise
as the landscape he has created
is revealed before his eyes?

Having nailed his mirror
in its place
firmly to the wall,
why the sudden tremor
at the sight of his own face?

Why the sudden terror
at the horror of it all?

"DOING THE SPIRIT OF GREAT SNAKE"

Before a would-be monk is ordained,
he is called Nāga (Great Snake).
Jain Narong (He Who Has Long Campaigned)
has come of age
and, for his grandmother's sake,
sits in the afternoon before his ordination
and waits for a drama to unfold.
He faces a table with a palm-leaf fan on
and wears a robe of brocaded white and gold.

There are no monks present.

Around the edge of the red carpet
is a three-sided circle (yes),
where thirty five people are set
(and one baby).
Outside the circle, a dozen (more or less),
hang around to see
what the outcome will be.

Nāga sits next to Doctor Spirit
and Lady Doctor Spirit.
She has been in a trance for half an hour,
hands pressed together,
body inclined towards the table with the flowers,
preparing for the occasion.
Nāga's parents sit behind.
His mother is gaunt and pale as a Caucasian;
enormous eyes in shadowed lids slide
restlessly from side to side.

The Band starts with a boom;
trumpets, trombones, boat-shaped gamelans,
a kong and two double-headed drums.
(It is a big band for a small room.)
Just as suddenly, it stops.

Doctor S begins chanting;
in the Indian style
(the meaning
is in the wailing).
The language is Pali
and though the sound
is shaped by syncopation,
there is a disregard for cadence

(and sense).
It is the language of magic and incantation
rather than instruction.

Next comes an Invitation to Devas of All Classes;
Devas from the planes of Sensual Pleasures,
Rupa Brahmas, Bhuma Devas,
Nature Spirits, Ether Devas,
Guardians of Treasures,
Yakkhas, Nāgas and Ghandarvas,
Devas from celestial mansions,
jungles, fountains,
rice fields, streams and rivers, mountains,
garden spirits and Chao Ti's,
all are invited to these festivities.

Devas, they say, like peace and solitude,
(they may also, of course, enjoy an *interlude*)
and such an all-inclusive invitation
to the universe's unknown, furthest stations
needs musicians who will do their best
to boom it where the deafest
Devas hide undisturbed.
How many have made it here? I cannot guess.
But Doctor S
seems satisfied
(and the baby unperturbed).

There is an unexpected hush.
I wondered what that golden bowl was for.
From it, Dr S takes a decorator's brush
and carefully paints Nāga's head,
neck and shoulders with water,
which he then splashes round the room.
Is this to cool us – it *is* unconscionably hot?
Or purify the room? Probably not.
More likely it's a signal
that the Performance will begin,
this drama Doctor S and Lady Doctor S are in.
They are both narrators and performers
and will give voice to the traumas
of spirits, which otherwise were dumb
and will, in Thai, speak for them
(and with high decorum)
every time they come.

Doctor S tells Great Snake the debt he owes

his parents, particularly his mother,
and goes on to propose
a review of Great Snake's life.
He says he'll start with day one in the womb
(that tiny, expanding single room).
Lady Doctor S wails and shrieks and groans
to express the discomfort, the confinement,
the mother's pains and premature contractions,
with the sympathy and encouragement
of gamelans, kong, trumpets and trombones;
and to everyone's apparent satisfaction.

The trombones blare, the drums boom louder.
The emotional temperature rises.
The metal keys of the gamelans
are hammered ever harder.
Lady D is inspired. She writhes, she agonises
in a most enthusiastic trance.
Two small boys, aged two and three,
jump on the monks' platform and dance.
Onto the red carpet, two women crawl
and offer money to Doctor S,
who takes it with no acknowledgement at all.
The birth pains become more intense
and the music goes full volume.
A group of girls start clapping their hands
in time to the kong and the gamelans
and swaying with excitement.
Two older women start beating the floor.
This is contagious and soon there are more.
A plump woman is bouncing
on her buttocks while bending her knees
and slapping her feet
to accompany the mother's agonies
and her clamouring
for exotic foods to eat.
At last, the climax is reached,
the midwife is sent for,
the waters are breached.
The girls wail hysterically,
the music blares apoplectically,
(the baby screams epileptically).

After fully forty minutes in the womb,
Great Snake is born,
to the immense satisfaction
of almost everyone in the room.

Great Snake himself
has shown no particular emotion
through all this commotion
and is no doubt practising *Detachment*
(the fourth Brahma Vihara) quite untainted.
His mother looks as though she has fainted
in a sitting position.

I decide it is time to move on.
For ninety minutes, fruit flies
have been trying to get into my eyes,
mosquitoes have been biting me,
I have been sharing my blood with a flea.
What is more, it now appears,
Great Snake's life has another twenty years
to run before his spiritual consummation.

Tomorrow, he will become
Jotipanno (Bright Wisdom).

ORDINATION

The next day, to clashing music and shouts,
Jotipanno is carried
around the Uposotha Hall
by yesterday's revellers
and deposited at the door.

Inside the Hall,
no revellers and no music.
On a raised platform
there is a notice banning women.
On a green carpet
sits the Preceptor
with incredibly tired eyes
and twelve powerful looking monks,
aged from forty-five to eighty-two;
a spiritual bodyguard
on the lookout for Māra.

Jotipanno asks to be a novice.
He is given ten precepts,
which he accepts, and changes
his white robe for yellow.

Now he asks to be a monk.
He is told to wait by the door
where two senior monks interrogate him.

Are you a human being?
Are you a man?
Are you in debt?
Are you on bail?
Do you have your parents' permission?

He has learned the responses by heart
for he speaks no Pali.
The interrogators are satisfied.
Jotipanno is led to the platform
to go through it all again
before the Preceptor
and the Spiritual Bodhi Guard.

Finally it is over.
Venerable Jotipanno leaves the Uposotha Hall
to a throng of relatives and well-wishers outside.
Each places a bundle of flowers and joss sticks

(and a brown envelope)
into his shoulder bag.
He wais his thanks.

*"You don't have to wai now,
 you're a monk already."*

Thirteen days later,
Jotipanno leaves the Sangha
and reappears in the world
disguised as a layman.
His grandmother, it seems, is satisfied.

NEW RECRUITS REPORT TO THE GUARDROOM

On Tuesday after a silence
of three months,
suddenly,
where the jungle
throws evening shadows over the bougainvilleas,
all the cicadas shouted out at once;
stretching and releasing their tymbals
like the shimmering and vibrating
of a thousand silver cymbals.

No notices were posted on the trees.
No announcements in the press.
No sergeant major shouted, "one, two, THREE!"
No ragged more or less.
Nothing in their diaries told them when to come.

They all march together to a single, silent drum.

THE CLOISTER AND THE HEARTH

The Venerable Ratanapanno
(Jewel of Wisdom)
of Wat Viharnhongdieow
(Vihara with one Room),
is forty-eight today.

The villagers say
he has been meddling with their women
and doing black magic for the men.
Abbot Sutin Thanadhammo has spoken;
pointing out the precepts he has broken.

Jewel of Wisdom has not allowed
vengeful thoughts to subside.
He has put poison
in the Abbot's coffee.
On March the ninth, the Abbot died.
The villagers say he is now in prison
and unlikely to get off free.

AWN (FLEXIBLE)

Awn is thirty, tall and thin.
He delivers gas bottles on a motorcycle.
He lays them across the pillion
and bends his left arm behind him
to hold them steady;
right hand steering,
accelerating,
braking,
over hump-backed bridges,
through left turns,
running the gauntlet of dogs.

For five thousand baht
and three days off a month.

On his free days,
his grandmother
comes from Bangkok
at five a.m. and takes
him back with her
to deliver cakes.

He supports:
his father's mother
(who drinks two bottles
of alcohol a day
and swears at the world);
his elder brother
(who is missing one leg below the knee);
his sister's two young children
(who are nine and eleven).

*"I have worked for eight years
  without a rise.
  I make merit at the Temple
  and chant the mantra
  before I go to sleep."*

DEBTS AND TAXES

At New Year,
Awn went out with Somchai,
his friend from Chiengmai,
who worked nearby
in Pinit's factory.
Five local boys who live by the lock
attacked Somchai.
They didn't mean to kill him
but when they stamped on his neck,
it snapped.
Awn knew them.
They were arrested.

As a surprise present,
Somchai's parents had bought
him a new pickup.
This has been sent
to Chachoengsao
to pick up his corpse.

The parents of the five
are still alive
and poor.
They have had to borrow
half a million baht.
Two hundred thousand goes to appease
the grief of Somchai's parents;
three hundred thousand goes to the police
for the boys' release.

The five have lost their jobs at the factory.

TWO TREES

Khun's house stands impermanently
by a large and ancient Bodhi tree.
This has lent him its shade
since the house was first made
and has spread its branches comfortably.
Under such a tree was Buddha enlightened.

Hundreds of birds come here
to nest,
to rest,
to watch the night fade
and the dark sun appear.

Khun has heard of chicken flu.
Seeing all those birds, he fears
that he might catch it too.
He drew the Council's attention to it.
He wanted the tree cut down
and the Council to do it.
The Council refused,
said no, declined, demurred.
But Khun was not so easily deterred
and hired a local man to do it for him.
But first he knelt down on the ground
(Suchit saw him).
He put his hands together
in a gesture of submission
and asked the Bodhi tree's permission.

I do not know
what the tree had to say
but I do know
it was chopped the very same day.

Opposite Wat Krathum,
a large and ancient banyan tree
has been blown down by the wind.
A Medium says the deva
has been complaining it is homeless.
On Sunday the old Headmaster (eighty three)
announced in the Temple
that local people had collected
seven thousand baht
for a large Spirit House to be erected
next to the stump.

LADIES FIRST (please)

Here in the GENTS,
leaning across the wash hand basin
to get a little nearer
to the mirror
she can see her face in,
pushing out her yellow boiler suit behind her
(she sees no reason why I should mind her),
a thirty year old woman is intent
on squeezing out spots with scarlet finger nails
in this haven where modern males
come to make themselves content.

Seeing my reflection
behind her beauty session,
she shows no recognition,
no recollection;
just a passive aggression
in the eyes
of someone very easily
not surprised.

KIK (RATTLER)

Kik is 26 years old.
She says she is
a good Thai girl, a virgin.
She has long hair died blond.
She makes and sells cheap fashion jewellery.
She pays 10,000 baht a month for her stall.
She lives with her parents and sister.
Her ambition is a farang boyfriend
and luk krung* children.
She has spent a month's rent
getting the bridge of her nose westernised.
She has good eyesight
and hazel-green contact lenses.
She keeps a wooden penis in her till
to bring her good luck.

How is it with you?
"Not good." (mournfully)
"Yesterday,
 farang come Big C.
 He tall, very handsome.
 Very Hi-Soh.
 My friend ask him, he like me?
 He say No.
 My face western.
 He want Thai girl,
 not Thai girl look western.
 I want to die."

*Luk krung; *someone with one Thai and one
western parent.*

MĀRA

Māra's bones
are carved as dice.
You can win once
but never twice.

POETRY

Poetry begins with pain
(like any other kind of birth)
but though it breeds and feeds on earth,
it aims at not becoming back again
and reaches to the roots of things
in search of the eternal springs.

MIDSUMMER DREAM

I dreamed of Paradise Garden;
sunlight sliding down
from an infinite sky
through cedar trees to emerald lawns;
oriental poppies six feet high,
Indian butterflies gliding by
through multilayered shades of blue.
Olympian Apollo's statue
holds a fountain in his hands,
which swirls and mists, sparkles and cools,
cascading down to deep green pools,
where red carp flash on silver sands.

Gazing round I find,
beyond the mirror of my mind,
past flowering trees and shrubberies,
how all around
this fertile ground
the garden is confined
within a fence of iron bars,
which stretches high
to arch across and make a canopy
between me and the sky.
The falcons, hawks and eagles
which circle round are kept at bay
and cannot swoop to seize as prey
the song birds that sing here all day.

Beyond the bars, a crawling multitude
swarms to and fro insatiably
but cannot find its way
into my garden solitude.

Heavens! I thought, the truth is clear to me!
That restless swarming world
is a prison shut *in* by iron bars.
Only I, in my garden, am completely free!

THE KING'S MINISTER

The King's Minister,
in the King's Pleasure Garden,
saw a leaf falling.
Just that.

And within it, all the other leaves
and all the other pleasure gardens
and all the other Kings
and all the other Kings' Ministers,
together with their lotus pools
and hand maidens
and singing birds
and magnolia trees
(and King's Ministers)
and the deafening
brown and yellow cosmic chant
of here today (King's Ministers)
and gone tomorrow (King's Ministers).
Just that.

Becoming a paccekabuddha, *
he rose up into the air
and flew off to the Himalayas.

Here the northwest wind
has stripped
the palms of their yellowed leaves,
and left the privet battered,
the marigolds bedraggled,
the daisies tattered;
has whipped
the wallflowers to crumpled cork,
the alyssum to dry powdered chalk.

Here the King's Minister's
smile is blithely sinister;
"In here, the wind can't bother me!"
He rings the bell for morning tea.

---

* Paccekabuddha: *Independently Enlightened One.*

ALL DONE BY MIRRORS

One man's yesterday
is another man's magic theatre;
in which he creates the past
he likes to think he had
and finds that things weren't quite so bad
(or even a good deal better).
He stretches out and bends
both time and place
and smooths the contours of each face,
the beautiful and the ugly,
to make or mould or find
a glove which fits
the deformed fist
of his mind
more snugly.

AYUDHAYA PERIOD 17ᵀᴴ CENTURY ANON

Rumbling rumbling.
Not thunder.
Elder Brother
groans.

Whirling whirling.
Not wind.
Elder Brother
wails.

Gushing gushing.
Not rain.
Elder Brother
weeps.

Burning burning.
Not fire.
Elder Brother
burns
with desire.

THE MEDIUM

Last evening a heavy crunching
on the gravel drive
between here and the river.
Ang and Dek are dragging a spirit house
through a moonless night.

What are you doing?

*"Can we throw this
into the river in front of your house?"*

Why?

"It is empty. Manit has bought a new one."

Why bring it here?

*"We can't leave it by the road.
Bad spirits move into empty houses
by the road and cause accidents."*

Drop it in the river by your house.

*"The bank is wrong.
It goes straight down.
Here the bank slopes.
It will slide down.
The river devas will take care of it.
There will be no danger."*

Tong Dee is thin
wears a yellow shirt,
has short hair.
However she puts her body,
it is uncomfortable.
For six weeks she has been a medium.
When she speaks,
it is with the voice of a spirit drifting
between death and rebirth,
trying to communicate with the living,
grasping at mother earth
with de-atomizing fingers.

It is making Tong Dee ill and thin.
Wek, her grandmother,

has invited a great Deva
to stop the spirits getting in.

Today, Tong Dee's mouth complained,
*"They have taken my house.
 I have nowhere to go."*

HUNGRY RIVERS

All rivers are hungry.
Bang Pakong is a river.
The Japanese built a multimillion-dollar dam
to keep the river out
when it turned salty in December
and let it in
when it became freshwater in May.
This has made it hungrier.
Saltily pouring in from the sea,
it hits the dam and rushing back,
meets itself head on,
spreads out in frustration
and eats the earth
one metre every year.
In front of us, orchards and five houses
have gone forever,
together with their spirit houses,
the spirits blown away into the void.

We approached the Prime Minister
and he was removed by a coup d'état.
We approached the Governor
and he was replaced by a new governor.
The new Governor said;
"Something must be done!
Urgently!
Top Priority!
And the old Governor had funds!"
But since the coup d'état,
it seems the funds have disappeared.
Coups d'état
are hungrier even than rivers.

The Governor gave the job to the Water Board.
Urgently. Top Priority.
And they have the funds.
Unfortunately, we cannot
give them the brown paper envelope
which contains the key
which unlocks the safe
where the funds are kept SAFELY.

But there has been correspondence
and meetings and dates
which came and went and left no trace

(a puzzle for Einstein
and the Conservation of Energy).

One day, unexpectedly and unannounced,
eleven cars made the gravel rumble
along the edge of the jungle
and parked under the lamut trees
and the coconut trees.
Out got twenty-five men
(feminism is unpopular here)
and three drivers (also men).
They wandered
among the jak trees
and the kak trees,
talking animatedly
and pointing at the river.
They seemed surprised to see it
just there.

Chao Nai (Mr. Big) had also come.
We never found out why he was called Mr. Big
nor where he had come from.
He stood quietly under a tamarind tree,
looking very short
and speaking Thai softly and politely.
His secretaries and the Engineer
stood with their hands crossed humbly
in front of them.
They too were big. But not BIG.
He spoke peacefully to Acharn Pisamorn.
Rivers, he suggested were, in fact,
just like that.
Acharn Pisamorn pointed to our house
which is now uncomfortably close
to a river which is, in fact,
just like that.
Mr. Big looked at the Engineer.
The Engineer understood that look.
Rivers, said the Engineer, move
not only up and down
but from side to side,
just like that.
He produced a map showing how much
the Bang Pakong had moved silently
(it was a quiet map)
side to side and westward
for a hundred years,

even before reacting violently
to being shut in (or out)
by a Japanese dam.

He spread out his map
under the tamarind tree.
Acharn Pisamorn knelt down to look.
Mr. Big saw this and,
with perfect manners, knelt too.
When the secretaries and the Engineer
saw Mr. Big on his knees,
they immediately dropped to their knees.
When the twenty other officials saw this,
they stopped being surprised
at the position of the river and knelt as one
(without even checking whether dogs
had passed this way recently).
Being more aware of the nature of dogs,
the drivers vanished behind their cars.
Acharn Pisamorn, oblivious
to this demonstration
of the power of oriental etiquette,
focused her concentration
on a graphic illustration
of the westward hunger
of the Bang Pakong river.
Mr. Big watched her peacefully.
Everyone else waited for Mr. Big to get up.
Or further down.
Hopefully not this last
since that honour
was normally reserved for the King
(and dogs *may* have passed...).
Acharn Pisamorn finished investigating
the mysteries
of flumenal history
and stood up.
Immediately (but afterwards)
Mr. Big stood up.
Immediately (but a little later)
twenty men stood up.
The drivers reappeared.

And that was that really.

Mr. Big peacefully (but seriously)
pointed out where the river

was waiting peacefully (but hungrily)
and explained that it was a matter of urgency
and top priority.
Everyone (in order of seniority)
hurried to pay
their respects to Acharn Pisamorn,
got into their cars and drove away.

Since that meeting
twenty five months have passed,
one month for each man
(not counting drivers).
Many of those who came have lost their jobs
or been transferred
by the Military Government.
The river has collected two tributes
and advanced two metres.
We are still not in a position
to put a key of the right denomination
in a brown envelope.

Had it been Mohammed Al Fayed,
a stream of brown envelopes
would have been going out in all directions.
By now the Bang Pakong river
would be incarcerated in a pipe
under an eighteen-lane concrete highway.

Think of what he did to the Conservative Party.

LUK CHANTANA

On the full moon eve
of the twelfth lunar month
the image of Luang Por Sothorn leaves
his Temple on a carved golden float
from which huge gilded nāgas stare out.
Chinese fireworks and cannon blast out.
Amplified epics blare out
the story of his journey from Ayudhaya.
Crowds of believers on their knees exhort him.
A flotilla of golden boats escort him.

Today, in one of them, came Luk Chantana
(Fruit of Sandalwood).
She is sixty-eight
with backward-looking eyes.
At thirteen, she went to see her brother,
a policeman living near Davi Vidyagun school.
She was taken by surprise
and needed to urinate.
Since she could not wait,
she was doing it discreetly
on the ground outside the gate,
when she saw a figure approaching rapidly.
When it reached her,
it disappeared inside her
and possessed her.

She had urinated
on the exact spot
where her brother's sister-in-law
had been killed
by a motor vehicle.

She became very ill,
her body covered in spots.
She babbled deliriously of the dead girl.
No-one could cure her.
They said her horoscope
had been broken.
The only hope
was Doctor Khi.
He might help her
if she had a karmic link with him.
But he would have to adopt her,
properly, legally,

and registered at the Amphur District office.

So it was done.
He treated her
and she was well again;
except for those backward-looking eyes
and the need to tell her pain
to each and anyone passing by.

Fifty-five years have gone
but only this
is what her thoughts dwell on.

BODY SNATCHERS

Under a bridge,
white van
blue overalls,
accident
black spot.

The spirits
of those who die violently
spiral around in turbulence,
causing more accidents.

The Buddhist Association,
funded by public donations,
collects the pieces
and pacifies the spirits
with chanting and cremations.

It is an unconnected fact
that, even if a body is not intact,
disconnected
body pieces
fetch good prices
in a global market.

This is the organic arm
of environmentally friendly recycling,
matching the end-buyer
with the finished product.

The catalogues are on the net.
A for Arm? That's what you get!

FLOWERS OF THE HUMAN SPIRIT

A woman looks up
from her place
among the dirt and pollution
of Silom Road and joins
her palms together in salutation.

Someone has put two one-baht coins
in her plastic cup
(without looking at her face).

One hundred yards away,
The British Club is going to cool
their swimming pool
with ice for a Polar Swim
at 11.00 a.m. on New Year's Day.
"Free of Charge. Free hot mulled wine."
(There is a double crash barrier
with uniformed security guards
to protect would-be polar swimmers.)

At the Bangkok Motor Show,
an as-white-as-snow
Bugatti Veyron is à la carte,
escorted by swirling girls
in white satin evening gowns.
253 mph top speed,
turbocharged, all souped-up.
To squeeze out
all its growling sounds,
you will need
to take 165 million baht

out of your plastic cup.

THANK YOU MR. EDISON

Jingle bells. Jingle bells
Jingle all the way.
Oh what fun it is to ride
On a one horse open sleigh!
Oh!

At the next bamboo table,
by a rustling opalescent sea,
four year old Bun,
armed with a red box
powered by two AA batteries,
is carving his private heaven
out of his familiar hell.
Continuously every five seconds.

After five minutes
it has repeated sixty times.
The neighbouring tables,
being teetotal,
are silenced.
The chairs uncomfortable.

After fifteen minutes
and one hundred and eighty repetitions,
the axe-head birds and birds of paradise
have given up.
Thais drinking mekhong
are murmuring in time,
if not in tune,
Jingen ben. Jingen ben.

After twenty minutes
and two hundred and forty repetitions,
the only competition
is the piped music
and the silver haired German
who is beating his wife
with airy gestures and
Ihre Tochter! Ihre Tochter! Ihre Tochter!

Fünf Minuten später,
Die Frau, too, is released
from her angst
by Santa's mechanical jingling;
her husband becomes speechless.

His fierce Teutonic eyes
which had imprisoned her attention
are neutralized by a four year old
with two AA batteries
and Thomas Edison's
patent number for a phonograph.

Only robotic piped music
can compete with a US patent.

A tropical restaurant
at the ocean's edge of paradise,
canopied by a full moon
and a transparent gauze of stars
provided by the Tropic of Cancer,
endures a public purgatory
provided by one boy's private sanctuary.

Unexpectedly, it is over.
A much younger sister
dashes Edison's legacy to the sand.
The shock is too much for the batteries.
The red box lies in the dust, silent.
The boy's cocoon is broken.
In rage he throws sand and fists at the girl.
In fury the mother slaps him down.
Only the piped music remains
to insinuate a little comfort
around two dozen bamboo tables
and ninety-six chairs.

"All happy families are the same.
Every unhappy family
is unhappy in its own way." *

* Tolstoy: the beginning of *Anna Karenina*

TAOIST SAGE

Four foot tall
grey goatee beard
sharp incisive eyes,
he squats each morning on the pavement
of Silom Road;
with his back to the eternal struggle
of bus and taxi,
with a plastic cup
collecting his alms round
of single baht coins.

His sense of humour is undeniable.
What merit do his benefactors reap?

SHE SAID...HE SAID...

Gossip and slander
is pouring water
on the earth.

A knife scraping a stone
does not bruise it.

Even Buddha images
are tarnished.

How can a man of earth
escape censure?

VIPĀKHA KARMA

"Last week,
I stole ten lumyai
from Tong Dee.

See! Today,
I have given her
half a pineapple.

Why should she complain?"

PHAK CHEE

From September to November
as the rains give way to the cool season,
boats cross the Bang Pakong
to abandon female dogs on this bank.
Presumably, Wat Koh Chan is full.

Phak Chee, the Doberman, is old.
Every night she has fought
the Black Ridgeback
which comes to the river bank
to howl across half a mile of water
to the place from which she was brought.

NGU HAU BIN KEOW

Mother Rabieb is ninety.
For as long as she can remember,
the singing cobra
(cobra with jewelled hairpin)
has come at late evening.

Geriiing geriiing geriiing
like tinkling brass.

ELEPHANTIASIS

Wrinkled, grey leg
twenty four inches wide
below the knee.

Every step
a heavyweight burden.

No complaint.
No expression on the face
as guide and driver
ease him clumsily
into a samlaw.

The street is full
of walkers
and hawkers
monks and policeman
upasikas and school children.

No-one notices.
Everyone has been taught;
this is karma which surfaces
if you kicked mother or father
in a former life.

JONG ANG

At 11.00 o'clock,
in Queen Sowabha's Snake Farm,
they extract the venom.
Visitors watch from tiered seats
as the cobras are carried out
and milked to make serum.

The farm is overfull.
Snakes are brought here
from all over the kingdom
in bags and boxes
and must not be turned away.

If you have been bitten
this is the place to come.
You are advised to bring the snake with you
to be sure of treatment with the right serum.
You are also advised to be quick.

In this cage are the king cobras.
The longest one ever recorded
was fished out of the Chao Phya river.
Usually all that is to be seen
are the smaller snakes
put in this cage to feed them.
One day I took Ben.
He has aroused kundalini
and used to dream of snakes.
He quite often meets them.

We stood and waited.
A long snake crossed the cage
very quickly, lifted its head
and displayed its hood.
I crouched down to eye level
and moved my hand from side to side
slowly like a pendulum.
The head swung in unison.
Gradually I raised the swinging hand
and myself until I was standing,
hand swinging before my face.
The snake had kept pace
with my hand and its head
was level with mine.
Side to side.

Silent rhythm.
Hand and head.

A fine and ancient head
set with two unmoving jewels.

I dropped my hand. Eye to eye.
Suddenly, it struck.

There are cobras that spit and blind
but the king's head
only hit the wire mesh
which bruised and bloodied its mouth.
Jong Ang struck twice more
before dropping down
and sliding away
into a water channel
with head erect.

KINGDOM OF HEAVEN

A poor man's thanks
come from his heart.

A rich man's presents
come from his pocket

and expect a return
above bank rate.

SĀLĀ CHAROOSOMBHAT

This large and splendid sālā was built
by the Police Chief and his brother,
the Deputy Prime Minister
in the ousted government.
Along one wall the monks sit and chant,
facing a suite of Chinese furniture,
four armchairs and a three-seater settee,
lacework carvings polished in the round.
The guests do not consider themselves
sufficiently distinguished to sit on these.
Nor do we, so we sit with all the rest
on rows of white plastic seats behind,
where we drink matoom,
gold, refreshing Bengal quince.

The floor tiles are grey, the walls white
and hung with coloured blankets,
which bear the donors' names.
After the funeral, these will be given to the poor.
The ornate white and gilt coffin
contains what Chom,
the village Headman's mother in law,
has left behind of the four elements,
air and earth, fire and water.

Suddenly, the Police Chief is here,
dressed in understated black,
which reveals gold flashing
when he waves his arms.
He walks comfortably about his sālā
shining on his guests,
making golden gestures.
Everyone seems pleased to be shined on.
When he sits in solitary splendour
on his seven-seater rosewood suite,
some of the guests offer him drinks,
so that they can drop to their knees
and be shined on even more brightly.
Such is the Power of Police Chiefs.

They have many subsidiary powers too.
One is the revolver hanging on their hips.
Another is the power of their visiting cards.
If you have one (the card, that is, not the gun),
you put it next to your driving license.

The next time you are pulled over
by a policeman, for speeding
or because he is collecting donations
to fulfill his quota of fines,
when he invites you to get out of your car,
you give him your driving license.
He looks at the visiting card and says,
"*You* know *this man?*"
Modestly, you say,
"*He is my neighbour.*"
Then, the form is this:
the policeman smiles beatifically,
stands to attention, salutes immaculately.
He stops the traffic so that you
can make your getaway smoothly.
I have seen this card at work.
Everything goes very well
and makes everyone happy
(except the driver of the car behind.
He will have to pay a double fine
to compensate for the shortfall
the magic card has caused).

The Police Chief was ten
when he last saw Acharn.
But he recognised her,
and came over to the plastic seats
and shined *up* at her (metaphorically).
He called her "Jay" (*Elder Sister* in Chinese).
He shook my hand and smiled.
He wished me *good morning* in English.
I smiled and wished him *good evening.*
(Was there a difficulty over GMT?)
We both smiled.
Honour was satisfied.
He led us to share his collection of chairs
and chatted with Acharn
until the monks started chanting,
their faces concealed by palm leaf fans.
*Wholesome deeds *
Unwholesome deeds
Neutral deeds.....

* *kusalā dhammā akusalā dhammā upekkhā dhammā.....*
The first three lines of Chapter 1 of the Abhidhamma.

When the chanting was over,
the Police Chief presented each monk
with a robe, flowers, joss sticks, candles
(and a brown envelope).
Someone brought Acharn
a tray with a gilt brass bottle.
From it she poured water carefully
into four gilt brass wine cups.
These were taken outside
and emptied onto the ground
so that Mother Earth would be able
to bear witness to an act of merit,
just as She had done at the moment
of the Buddha's Enlightenment
under the Bo Tree
when she had drowned Māra's army.

Then the Police Chief and Acharn
continued their recherche du temps perdu
until he put something in her hand
and invited us to his house
the next day, after the burning
of Chom's ninety-three year old body.

Invitations from Police Chiefs
are nothing special.
They are the same as invitations
from ordinary policemen
to get out of your car
so that he can search it for illegal weapons,
drugs or excuses to fine you.
Generally, out of courtesy,
you accept these kinds of invitation.
So we accepted (out of courtesy).

"What did he give you?" I asked.
She opened her hand.
There in silver lettering
on white card, was set out
the contact details
of a Police Major General.
"He said to phone his mobile
 if we needed anything."

"Does he know about your elopement?"

"Oh yes! Everybody does."

AMPHAI (RADIANT)

went to Trad near Cambodia
and caught malaria.
Her fever was very high.
She thought she was going to die.
Four Red Men led her
to a settlement of dwellings nearby
where she recognised dead relatives.
Whatever they wanted
materialized before them.
When they were alive,
said the Red Men,
they did meritorious deeds.
She was taken to another settlement.
The tables were piled high with food
but no-one here could eat or drink
because they hadn't given alms
of food and water to the monks.

The four men led her
back home.
They said her
time had not yet come.
The door was closed.
"Call mother," Amphai said.
But the men in red
passed silently in through the door.
She saw her body lying on the floor.
She entered it and asked her mother
for water and a mango.
Then she felt the fever go.

Her husband Thep
has left her to stay in a monastery
near Uthaithāni,
the city of sunrise.
The old Abbot has told him not to go
outside the temple gate
because his karma is lying there in wait.
Last week while he was walking
under the big trees, everything
became quiet and still
and a large branch fell,
splitting the back of his head,
causing his blood to be shed.
He is very mindful now.

PRATHEUNG AND THE MONKEY

Pratheung, the Enhancer,
had a monkey.
She loved it very much
and let it sleep on her bed.
When it died she was very sad.
Soon she became pregnant
and when Bom was born,
she said it was her monkey
coming back to her.
She gave the baby to her younger sister,
who was seventeen, to look after
and went to teach in another province.
Bom is eight now.
When Pratheung is not working,
she spends her time buying plants
and looking after her garden.

*"I would rather
grow flowers
than children."*

THE PENDULUM

There are monthly health assessments
upstairs in Sun's Health Food Shop.
You pay 100 baht* on arrival.
Forty-three people are waiting,
including two monks and three nuns.
These are invited to jump the queue.

My back is hurting.
I place my right hand
upside down with the fingers curled
on the table between us.
Acharn Suddhivas (Pure Rain)
dangles a pleasant looking
torpedo shaped pendulum,
hanging from a heavy silver watch chain,
above the base of my first finger.

My hand begins to tingle.
"Electrons," says the Acharn.
"Your vertebrae
are out of alignment.
It affects your stomach.
Put a gold ring
on the index finger of your left hand.
You should not do shoulder stands.
Your liver is not good,
wear a silver ring
on the ring finger of your left hand.
Eat three-mushroom dom yam.
Every morning at seven
drink blended kaprao."

Downstairs again, I am led into a small room
with a grubby mattress on the floor.
I lie on it and the Acharn's son
forces my vertebrae, section by section,
painfully back into place.
I sit on a chair
and he lifts me up by the head.
"Your back will be all right
  in three or four days."
It has been hurting badly

---

* 100 baht = approximately £1.50

for four weeks now,
so that sounds good news.
"Thanks. How much do I owe you?"
"You have already paid."

Next morning, blended kaprao
is murky green and tastes delicious,
like a mixture of peppermint and basil.

I do believe my back
is a *little* bit easier.

MÈRE RABIEB

In the early hours of Sunday,
a nok saek* landed on the roof
and gave a single harsh shriek.
Rabieb died at 11.50 on Monday.
Her granddaughters in England
awoke, independently, at exactly that time.
In the evening, monks came and chanted:
Impermanent indeed
are conditioned things.
Arising and passing away
is in the nature of things.
Having arisen, they pass away.
Those who reach peace and calm are happy...**.
Her body lay in the house all night.

The next day she was offered
breakfast and lunch,
filled up with bottles of formaldehyde,
taken to the Temple
and spread out on a table.
Rosewater was poured
on her hand in a purification rite
and she was offered fruit.
Her mouth was distorted
when someone tried
to force her false teeth in it
to make her look normal.
She was put in a giltwood coffin
lined with gold imitation
Chinese banknotes.

The funeral lasted nine days.
Every evening food was provided
for the guests' bodies,
chanting for their minds,
a small piece of red thread for their safety
and brown envelopes for four monks.

  * Nok saek: *the screech or barn owl. When this happens,*
    it is believed that there will be a death in the house.
** *Aniccā vata sankhārā*
   upādavaya dhammino
   upajjitavā nirujjanti
   tesam vūpasamo sukho.

They sat and chanted
behind palm fans,
each with a different message
written on it in Thai;

Go Not Return
Sleep Not Wake
No Come Back Again
No Escape.

The seventh day
was another day of giving
breakfast to the monks.
Fruit was offered to the dead
(then taken home and eaten by the living).

On the Cambodian borders,
bodies cannot be burned on Mondays.
They call it "Ghost eat Ghost Day"
and believe the death will be followed
by another in the same family.
But, after some discussion,
it was decided we are not
on the Cambodian borders
and are anyway more enlightened.

We also, it seems, have a heightened
sense of ceremony
(or what might be called propriety).
On Monday a Royal Fire
to light the funeral pyre
was brought in a tin box
under police escort from Bangkok
and received by two long rows
of white-uniformed civil servants
with gold epaulets and medal ribbons.

Imitation white sandalwood flowers
were thrown on the coffin
and it was torched. Royally.
All who came were given a parasol
on which was written
"sum shade umbrella".

Finally, on Tuesday, breakfast
was given to the monks.
Afterwards they chanted

and undisguised *white* envelopes
were laid individually
in front of each one of them.

In this small, provincial, third world town,
this funeral for a ferryman's widow
who had sold vegetables
cost three thousand pounds
(not including brown and white envelopes).

You can burn
three old ladies
for that in England.

UNDERTAKER

Saeng (Light) is forty two.
"When I was twenty five, I died."
Four men in white with red caps
led him away along a gravel road.
On either side were sālās,
evidence of his good deeds.
At the end of the road were monks
and he gave alms to them.
The men in white said it was not yet his time
and he could go home.
He walked back alone
and the path was covered
with thorn needles.
He saw his body surrounded
by relatives dressed in white.
They had put his hands together
as a sign of respect for the Triple Gem.
They had bought a coffin
but were pleased
when they saw he was still alive.
He never told them his story,
"They would not understand it".
He made an adhitthāna: *
"In future, I will do only good karma."
He has been working
as an undertaker ever since.
*"Since then I truly believe there is karma
and the result of karma.
If anyone cannot afford a funeral
or a coffin. I pay for it myself."*
The Thais say that twenty five
is a crucial age.
You can go either way.

* adhitthāna; *resolution.*

THE WAY

The stepping stone path
runs across the valley.
Either some of the stones have sunk
or the mud has been rising.
Those who try to cross get muddy feet.
Some wander off.
Some sink and disappear altogether.

JUNGLE

Dark, tangled, still, very quiet;
nipa palms, krathin,
tamarind, banyan, coconut,
crawling rattan, creepers.
Impenetrable.
One evening, a large python
slid out and across the track
towards the river.

*"Forty years ago, this was an orchard.
Just there, was a mound
with a great camachili tree on top.
My father's grandfather was buried there.
A Chinese from China,
he was not cremated.
Later, when they levelled the mound,
they found no body,
just a white cobra.*

*A servant hanged herself in the outhouse.
After that the children moved away.*

*When Father and Mother died,
we never came back to live here.*

*Somewhere,
in there
is the house."*

DANCE OF THE SPIRITS

The invitation is in elegant sepia Siamese script
on very pale pink card with embossed borders.
  "All disciples and honourable guests
      are invited to join
      in paying respects
      to the Teachers."
The teachers are unusual though:
      Great Teacher Rishi
      Grandfather Wealth
   His Royal Highness Love Flower
      Chao Poh Dhamthamin
  Chao Poh the Black and Ruthless
      Chao Mère Golden Champa.
All of them are dead
but they will be there
for they are spirits.
His Royal Highness is a son
of King Chulalongkorn
who drowned, when he was ten,
in the sea near Bangsaen.
These spirits are devoted to helping people.

Pranom's mother had been their medium.
When she died, they moved to Pranom instead.
On Sunday, at the House by the Temple Wall,
breakfast for the monks is at seven,
respects to the Teachers at nine,
lunch at twelve.

Downstairs, under the house,
fifty people are waiting
and excitedly talking.
Are you going up?
"Oh, no. Oh no!"
They laugh.

Upstairs, fourteen mediums,
including Pranom (The Conciliator)
are changing into costumes.
There are six musicians,
with a ranard, two big drums,
one small drum and brass chings.

Along one wall are shelves.
On the top shelf is a large effigy

of Great Teacher Rishi,
hair tied up, long grey beard,
wearing a tiger skin robe.
Under him, tiers of images, mostly male
with some small children.
These are all tutelary spirits
who possess the bodies of the mediums.
The lowest shelf has an elaborate decoration
of banana leaves and flowers.
On the floor, a big smouldering,
clay joss stick holder.
Behind it kong wai (offerings)
of cakes, drinks and fruit.
Along the opposite wall, the monks
have sat, eaten their breakfast,
chanted a mantra bestowing merit
on the donors and departed.
About twenty "disciples and respectable people"
are watching the mediums change.
Pranom is local, the rest from other districts.
One dresses all in red, two in gold.
An old man appears as an Ayudhaya soldier.
He speaks entirely in rhyming verse.
Most are in white, old-fashioned Thai style.
Many are plump and middle-aged.
One girl, all in red, is in her late teens.
She is the medium for Sung Thong
(The Golden Conch Shell). *
Pranom begins. She takes one joss stick
and concentrates her attention on it.
The musicians play, two of them chant
mantras which evoke spirits.
Pranom is sitting cross-legged.
She starts to sway round and round
violently and erratically
like an unbalanced top.
She stops swaying and sits erect
before jumping eighteen inches straight up
and falling back on her plump
haunches with a great thump.

* *In Indian Legend, a Queen gave birth to a conch shell. The King's minor wife was jealous of this and bribed the court astrologer to say it was a bad omen. It was banished by being thrown into a river.*
Later, a Prince emerged from it who, after many adventures, became King himself and ruled justly and wisely.
The story is told in a Thai poem written by King Rāma II.

She is fat and bounces,
bang, bang, bang.
Her movements get wilder
as the musicians play louder
until she flops down on her face.
Great Teacher Rishi has arrived.
She takes seven candles,
holds them tightly together and lights them.
The flames flare up like a great torch
which she plunges into her mouth.
This is the signal
for the other mediums.
They sway demonically,
bounce incredibly
high on their middle-aged haunches,
and finally flop forwards or backwards
when the spirits come.
They light candles. They swallow flames.
All the joss sticks in the clay pot are alight
and, with the candle smoke,
create a thick haze in which the mediums
dance round the room
in time to the boom-boom
of the musicians,
stopping every few steps
to pay respects to each other.
The crashing, the banging, the noise
confirm the fears of all those beneath the floor
who had not dared to come up
but could not bear to keep away.

Pranom receives the first believer,
an old man with a half-crazed look.
Great Teacher Rishi's voice grates out,
"You cut trees down didn't you?"
The man nods humbly.
*"Don't you know that in those trees
there were devas?
That's why they've made you mad.
You saw two men standing there, didn't you?"*
"Yes."
*"Get them a spirit house.
Then you will be all right."*

A big man, from another province, is next.
*"You got what you wanted, didn't you?
Boss of the Coca Cola Company*

in Rayong now, aren't you?"
The man smiles and bows.

Suddenly, one of the mediums
calls out that the Cripple is coming.
She crouches and writhes
(and swallows fire.)
The other mediums come and pay their respects.

All the mediums are receiving devotees
But the music is so loud
it is impossible to hear what is said.

By now the Prince
has replaced the Rishi in Pranom.
she comes over and a child's voice asks,
"When are you going back?"
I don't know.
*"You have an advantage over lots of people,
 living in two countries.
 May you be well, happy and rich."*

After two-and-a-half hours,
the spirits leave.
The mediums start to change
into ordinary clothes.
We go over to a warrior in red,
an attractive girl in her mid-twenties.
She is smoking
two cigarettes at once
which she is holding
between the index
and middle fingers of one hand.

How does it feel?

*"That is too broad a question.
 Be more specific."*

Who are you?

*"Many: Brahma, Siva, Naraya.
 Our purpose is giving
 without expecting anything in return.
 Give with the giving heart.
 To do this you need
 to be well established*

*in morality and Dhamma.
Those who drink alcohol and smoke
cigarettes are not wrong."*
Really?
No answer.

We went downstairs.
Lunch was beginning.
On our way out,
we were given five bags
of food and fruit.

At half past four,
lunch was still being eaten.
Late in the evening,
music could still be heard.

NEW YEAR'S DAY

All Uposotha Days are equal.
Those that fall
on New Year's Day
are more equal.
After the monks have finished breakfast,
they chant for longer than usual.
They chant the Karaniya Mettā Sutta,
the Ratana Sutta, the Mangala Sutta.
A white string links the Abbot, the monks
and the large gilded Buddha image in the corner
to a silver-plated pot of water.
Candles have been placed on the rim
of the pot, inclining inward.
During the chanting of the mantras
there is the drip drip of candle wax.
In this way the water itself becomes
Buddha Mantra Water
and is used to ensure everyone
gets a fair share of the merit.
This is particularly valuable
for those who cannot understand
the Pali words and might otherwise
get nothing out of it at all.
The Abbot picks up a broom head
made of a cluster of bamboos.
Carrying the bowl, he walks around the sālā
dipping his broom and enthusiastically
splashing the delighted devotees
whose karma is good enough
for them to be drenched.

The karma of my Jermyn Street shirt
is good enough to be missed.
I am delighted it remains quite dry.

YESTERDAY'S CHILDREN

Acharn Suphot is the Temple Warden.
Previously he was Headmaster
of the Temple School for thirty five years.

"In the past, for as long
as anyone can remember,
children studied the Code of Good Conduct.
Thirty years ago, the Government
appointed a Christian
as Minister of Education.
Soon after that, the Code of Good Conduct
was taken out of the schools.
That has been the case ever since."

What was wrong with the Code?

"Nothing. Listen.
A good person has proper respect.
A good person shouldn't be noisy
   where others are peaceful.
A good person doesn't use harsh language.
A good person has a sharing heart.
A good person doesn't think only of himself.
A good person dresses respectably.
A good person isn't aggressive with his words.
A good person doesn't interfere in others' affairs.
A good person respects all religious places.
A good person is respectful and polite to his seniors...
   You see? Things like that."

These are Thai virtues. Buddhist virtues!

"Yes."

And they produce a stable society?

"Exactly!"

SAMANASAKDI

Twenty five years ago the Committee,
led by Acharn Suphot, the Temple Warden
and Doctor Kim, the Head of the Village,
in accordance with the regulations,
proposed that the Abbot
should receive the honour
of the rank of Samanasakdi.
This is not a rank known to the Buddha.
But here, where teachers
and civil servants all have ranks,
just like soldiers and policemen,
it has become the custom.

The Acharn and the Doctor
took the customary flowers and joss sticks,
presented them to one
of the Kingdom's senior monks
and made their request.
He accepted the offerings
and acknowledged their request.
They went away.
Nothing happened.
They went twice more.
On the third occasion,
the senior monk said,
"*If you have money, you should use it
in a profitable way to get what you want.*"
The Acharn and the Doctor were astounded
and asked him what he meant.
"*Thirty thousand baht.*"
They wrestled much
with their consciences
and paid up.

The senior monk got £600.
The Abbot got a new name.
The Acharn and the Doctor face
a rematch with their consciences.

REFRIGERATION BLUES

Lek is the daughter of See.
Thirty-five years old,
with a ten-year-old son
she has worked
in a refrigerator factory
for thirteen years.
She stands four hours,
has half an hour for lunch,
stands four hours,
is taken home.
For two weeks she stands by day,
for two weeks she stands by night.
Plump.
Legs filling up.

She earns £25 per week.

HAUT CUISINE

The road to Lat Krabang!
On both sides, coconut trees lining;
beyond, emerald green rice fields shining.

Among the debris by the road
and the tumble-down huts,
roofed with grey-brown jak fronds,
are hand-written notices:

Already roasted rice field rats 70 baht each
Already roasted cobras 100 baht each.

CANDLE IN THE VOID

A glowworm there
on the mosquito screen.
They are not often seen
and have become quite rare.

WAT SUTAT

The English is impeccable,
the meaning unmistakable:

*"Please be advised
when in the sanctuary,
the intimacies between
a man and a woman
should be avoided."*

The Temple was built by Rama1
in his new city of Bangkok
to symbolize the centre of the Universe,
complete with the Sunantha Pool
and Suan Chitrlada,
the Palace of Indra.
Golden stepped ceramic roofs
are towered over by the Giant Brahmin Swing
and an even higher
red and white television mast.
White walls are lined with cloisters
in which classes of schoolchildren
are spaced out and being taught
Buddhadhamma by the monks;
(and one class of spaced-out older schoolgirls,
each in her teenage attitude,
who arrange and re-arrange their hair
and turn their heads and yawn and stare
in mid-morning lassitude).

Parquet marble paving
surrounds rectangular islands
of bonsai, koi and Natal plum,
cut into shapes
just as they appear
on Chinese porcelain.
A solitary swallowtail possesses
the long low pink needle hedges.
On the lawns, spreading Spanish cherry
and mango trees cast long shadows.
Ginnaris hold gas lamps and balance *
on ornate nineteenth-century iron posts.
The bases are cast as lotus flowers
on which Indra, cross-legged in a medallion,

*Ginnaris: *beings half-human, half–bird.*

floats above Erawan,
the three-headed elephant.

The Vihāra is full of old women in black
mourning for a dead princess.
They are listening to a sermon
on the three opportunities
in a human life;
wealth external,
wealth internal,
wealth eternal.

In the Preaching Hall,
the Buddha image
has been cast
from opium canisters,
confiscated during the reign of Rama Third.

Everywhere there is chanting
in praise of the Buddha
the Dhamma and the Sangha;
everywhere the sound
of teaching and sermons.

Everywhere, that is,
except where I now sit,
in the shade,
on the steps
of the Uposatha Hall.

Music is being played here, too.
But, unmistakably, it is Greensleeves
without the lyrics.
Discreetly,
I provide them myself.
*"Alas my Love you do me ill
 to treat me so discourteously."*

I look around.
No, there is no sign
of Henry Tudor
among the black dresses
and saffron robes.

TAXI DANCE

The surface deteriorated,
the samlaw in front of me
bounced around
on three wheels
all over the road
trying to avoid the potholes.
I drove up close behind it.
The hand-painted
Thai characters
on the back read:
*"However big,
  still smaller
  than a coffin."**
I lifted my right foot.

Smooth black tarmac again,
alive with mirages.
I accelerated past and away
until one of the images
didn't fade but became
a long section of light brown earth,
edged in blue, blocking my side of the road.
I went to drive straight over it
then, remembering
the infinitely expanding coffin,
I slowed down.

The farmer sitting on his haunches
looked up at me without expression
and returned to his task
of watching the rice
he had spread out
on a blue plastic sheet
dry evenly on the hot tarmac.

* *Yai taurai yang lek kwa long*

WAT SRAKET

This narrow bridge
crosses the Great Nāga Canal
to the gate of Wat Sraket.
The two sides are decorated
with lions and garlands of jasmine
and panels inset with life-sized figures
of sorrowing adults with children
in Ayudhaya-style clothing.
This is the Bridge of Tears.

In the reign of Rāma the Second,
there was a major
outbreak of cholera.
Families carried their dead
over this bridge
to the Temple charnel woods *
where they waited,
to be cremated.
Their clothes were taken
to be washed and stitched,
dyed with jackfruit juice or saffron
and recycled as monks' robes.
So many died that the long wait for cremation
resulted in a continuous demonstration
of the many stages
of decay and putrefaction.
Subjects like this for asubha meditation**
are hard to find.
Monks came from far away
to sit for hours and stare
at the shapes of Nothing there
and recreate in their minds
a counterpart image of the sign
of your destiny and mine.
This they took back to the loneliness
of their cells to contemplate
loathsomeness and impermanence
and break the bonds that attach
us to our humanity.
Sometimes, as they watched,

* charnel woods: *woodland within a temple compound where bodies were left, sometimes for years, waiting to be burned.*
** asubha: *not beautiful; loathsome.*

the corpse seemed to sit up
and reach out its hands.
In terror monks leaped
out of their cell windows
or lost their sanity.
A teacher who was an adept
stayed near at hand
so that the monk's life
might not be lived in vain.

During the Second World War,
many were killed in Allied air raids.
Once again, bodies decayed
while waiting to be burned
and monks came with resolution
to practise what they had learned
and fix these images of dissolution
as nimittas at the mind's door.*

The temple was built before
the destruction of Ayudhaya
and restored by the Chakri Dynasty
with a great golden pagoda in its grounds
to symbolize the centre of the universe.
As we climb towards the summit
loudspeakers relay a sermon;
*"Do not waste the treasure
 of a human life.
 Māra casts his net.
 The three āsavas corrupt* **
 the man, the family, society".

I climb past sets
of bronze hanging bells
engraved with verses
in praise of the Triple Gem.***
The steps are covered
with yellow flowers and petals
of Lanthom, the Tree of Sorrow.
Here is a notice:

  * nimitta: *mental image seen with the inner eye.*
  ** three āsavas: *three corruptions of sense desires, the desire for existence and ignorance.*
*** *The Buddha, his Teaching and his Order of Monks.*

*"If you want to be beautiful,
if you want to be attractive,
sweep the Temple paths."*

The loudspeaker is describing
how Moggallāna
defeated a fierce and powerful Nāga
named Nandapananda
whose head he had accidentally
sprinkled with dust
while flying across the Himalayas.

The last flight of steps
before the Golden Mount
is dusted with the transparent,
discarded wings of last night's flying ants.

At the top I go to lean against a wall.
I'm tired but that's irrelevant.
The fact is that I stumble
and dislodge a wooden elephant,
one of a pair that guards the doorway.
It clatters to the floor,
then down the steps it tumbles
in inelegant
free fall,
breaking up at every bounce
and, following the curve of the stairway,
the separating tusks and torso
this elephant has now become
disappear from view.

The security guard stands in my way.
I put my hand into my pocket.
How much *do* you have to pay
for a two-foot high elephant guardian
which protects a Golden Mountain?
And who do you think might stock it?

The loudspeaker intones its liturgy
*"All things are impermanent.
All things are unsatisfactory.
All things are not-self."*

The guard looks at not-elephant.
He smiles.
"Never mind! Never mind!"

Here under the golden dome,
the floor is freshly swept,
believers have come
to where the relics are kept.
They pay their respects,
make resolutions,
and requests
for health and happiness.

These are relics of Buddha himself,
dug up at Kapilvastu
by an Englishman,
together with provenance.

After his parinibbāna
and cremation,
the Buddha's earthly remains
were divided into eight portions
and shared among the Kings.
Those here are identified
as the portion given
to the Buddha's own clan
the Sakyans.

The Viceroy of India
gave them to King Chulalongkorn.
The King repaid this gift
by paying for Buddha's spiritual remains
to be published and translated
from Pali into English.

Which was the greater gift?

Brahma Sahampati provides the clue: *
*"There are those among gods and men
  with but a little dust in their eyes.
  They will understand the Dhamma too."*

---

* *After Buddha's Enlightenment, He was disinclined to teach, believing that no one would understand. It was this Brahma who, reading his thoughts, came down and persuaded him otherwise. Buddhists are greatly indebted to this Brahma. To this day, before a Monk delivers a sermon, a layperson will formally acknowledge this debt (in Pali).*

ĀMISAPŪJĀ

"Ah Koh Lai was my Grandmother.
She was a great devotee
and kept back the best
fruit for the alms round.
She hoarded up her money for the Temple.
When the rice plants
were pregnant with milk
in the young grains,
she would cut strips of plain white cloth.
She dyed them
in turmeric and water.
She tied them
on bamboo poles
and made yellow banners.
She planted one in each rice field.
She stuck a post in the ground
with a plate on top
and piled it with food and fruit.
Then she would light jossticks
and respectfully invite Mère Pho Sop *
to come and receive her offerings."

*Mère Pho Sop: *The Rice Goddess.*

AFTERNOON NAP

The Mère Ka sleeps peacefully
at three in the afternoon.
Her stall is on the corner
and the market is full of noise,
car fumes and decay.
Every day she comes from Prachinburi
and sells the fruit
her neighbour grows
without chemicals or pesticides.
Her papayas and jackfruit are very good.
Every day she comes.

She has paid to educate her daughter
through high school
and medical school.
Now her daughter is a GP.

The boy stands up to serve us,
"Don't disturb her. She is tired.
She gets up at two every morning."

BOA*

Sun and Da built a new house
of wood and tiles
and friendly smiles.
They opened it as the first and only
Health Food Shop
in Chachoengsao.
It was their home.
When their only child Boa was ten,
they sent her to a boarding school
in New Zealand.
"South Island."
Now she is fourteen.
*"I didn't know much English
I was very unhappy."*
Her accent is almost American,
sentences ending on a rising tone.
*"I was so lonely.
I meditated every day".*
How?
*"I stared straight ahead
at Nothing.
I used to write everything in my diary.
But now I have a friend
and I tell her everything.
I read all the time.
I've read all of Harry Potter.
Book Four is the best. And Book Seven.
I've read Book Four three times."*
In Thai?
"No, in English."
Don't you have trouble with the vocabulary?
The difficult words?
She looks at me in surprise,
the question is absurd.
*"Oh, no! I tried it in Thai
but somehow it's not the same."*
She speaks Thai with a foreign accent,
except when talking on the phone.
*"Mom and Dad want me to learn Chinese.
But they don't teach it at school.
I'm helping out in the shop
until Term starts.
Then I have to go back."*

*Boa: *lotus.*

*I play netball and basketball.
Netball's boring.
You just stand still
and you can't, you know,
go close to anyone."*
She waves her arms to show
just how close
to anyone
you can't go.
"But basketball is fun."

MĀRA'S SMILE

Māra's smile
is sweet and charming,
his eyes are actually quite disarming.
They shine on you in a sensual way,
eyes of a minor god at play.

A benevolent Al Capone
who will always send a cart to meet you
and help you carry your few belongings
when your latest foreign landlord
has thrown them after you on the street
and told you to go.
There is a flatness in his profile
as though cut out from the magazine *Hello*
and superimposed on his own shadow.

He is the Good Shepherd who aims to keep
his faithful sheep half asleep,
enturbulated in their dreams,
a kaleidoscopic collage of is and seems.
Pleasures and passions,
screams and wild laughter,
the Triumph of Life
and its morning after
are on his menu,
which he would share with you and you.
In Benares he has three daughters.
In Greece one, Circe, was all he needed
to entice you from your Wisdom
and ensnare you in his never-ending dance;
that long drawn out orgiastic trance
which squeezes out the last drops
of the living treasure you have saved.

When all your cells
are dried and emptied,
desires exhausted,
emotions corrupted
and bankrupted;
when you can no longer remember
what it's all about
nor keep your place or feet,
he'll shovel you out
onto the bald, blank street.

HIGH BLOOD PRESSURE

*"Does it say anything in your book
about high blood pressure?"*
It says forward bend, pranayama,
meditation and corpse position.
*"I do all that.
I go to bed before my husband
and say "Buddho".
I don't have a watch or a clock
so I count the Buddhos on my fingers
until he comes and turns out the light."*

NURSE

How was your day?

I started my work
as HIV Patients' Care Nurse.
I was Group Leader for stretching.
We finished at noon.
They got their medication
in the afternoon.
I had a new research title:
"Factors effect to HIV patients
for monthly hospital coming."
So I prepared myself
for being a safe sex
in Valentine's Day lecture tomorrow.

DOCTOR

I went to prison as usual.
The police took me to examine the man
who hanged himself last night.
His friends found him at three o'clock.
He stopped his medication
before he committed suicide.
We guessed he had a psychotic problem.
I had a walk and a run in the hospital.
I washed Annie's hair
before I went to bed.

MAKHA PUJA

A group of monks in Kornburi
went into the forest to meditate.
They set up their umbrellas
and started walking meditation.
Left goes thus.
Right goes thus.
A group of elephants attacked them.
One monk was seriously injured.
One climbed a tree.
One was trampled to death.

Fitness Trainer Amnart (Power) said,
*"They probably didn't have
 a protection mantra."*

The elephants had four babies.

GOOD MASTER GOOD SERVANT

Supaporn has restored her old family house
for half a million.
She lives there.
Ang cleans it.
She has built a new European house
for two million.
Her husband lives there.
Ang cleans it.
She has built a new traditional Thai house
for ten million.
Her mother lives there.
Ang cleans it
and looks after Supaporn's mother.
Supaporn has protected
her land against the river
for three million.
She has filled the land with plants
and lets Ang water them.
She has bought a new four by four Honda
for two million.
She has converted it to natural gas
for economy.
She drives it.
Ang does not drive it;
but she shops and cooks
and washes and irons.
Sometimes the children help Ang
by shouting at her.
But sometimes they don't help her.
She has built a wall to keep her neighbours out
and a kuti* above the water tank
from which she can watch her neighbours.
She pays Ang 3000 baht per month.

Recently Ang had cancer of the womb.
Her husband said, *"You are no use to me now!"*
and left her for a Cambodian immigrant.
Keyhole surgery for cancer removal
costs forty thousand.
Supaporn kindly lent Ang the money.
She said Ang could pay it back monthly
out of her wages.
Interest free.

*kuti: *a small hut especially one used for meditation.*

Toyota have built a factory
some distance away,
part of it on fields
bought from Supaporn.
They have kindly paid her
two hundred million.
They would kindly like
to buy some more, please.

TEMPLE BEGGAR

Dee is sixty two.
Somnuk is his sister.
Muee was his mother,
she was Chinese.
When Dee was twenty,
he saw his girl friend
talking to another man.
A gun was fired
and his shirt was torn.
Since then he has never worked.
His shirt and shorts
are forty years old,
dirty and tattered and reveal
more than they can conceal.
He begs at the Temple gate
and sweeps the dust and leaves.

"Give me five baht. Give me five baht."

People used to give him clothes.
Saisamorn used to give him ten baht.
One day she said,
"Why don't you wear clean clothes?"
"If I did, no-one would give me money."
After that Saisamorn ignored him.
Somnuk says he has lots of clothes.
He carries buckets of water
on a yoke from the Temple pond
to Somnuk's house.
He is emaciated and dirty
and his hair is dyed black.

"Give me five baht. Give me five baht."

JAI ING

Jai Ing has nine children
and no miscarriages.
She has a small wooden house
by the river Bang Pakhong
and a husband in the house
who has never worked.
He has two names:
his official name is Prayok, *
his nickname is Doo. **
Jai Ing made a living by catching
siew fish at night,
using a fine net and a lamp,
and selling them from her boat.
Her eldest son is Yongyudh.
He has many wives.
When Guk (Little Chick) was born,
Yonyudh's first wife left him.
She took the newborn baby to the lock
and asked a girl there to carry it a mile
and leave it under Jai Ing's house.
Jai Ing heard the baby crying
and climbed down the wooden stairs.
Since then she has looked after Guk.
Guk is twenty-seven and calls her "mother".
She designs ladies' underwear.
Yongyudh means "Eternal Battle".
Siew fish are about an inch long.
When Jai Ing gives alms on Uposatha Days,
she shares the merit with the siew fish.

* Prayok: *a sentence (grammatical).*
** Doo: *a cake made by roasting leftover rice.*

NA-KHUN SPEAKS

After the morning chanting,
the sermon.
A Preta* with a long body and a pig's head
appeared to Moggallana
and also to the Buddha.
Buddha explained; the Preta
had been greedy in a former life.

After the sermon,
Na-Khun declaims: "*See!
There is no escape from Karma!*"
She is eighty-four and smiles.
Nine old ladies agree.
With satisfaction.

"*Remember Eeoh!*"
Nine old ladies remember Eeoh.
With satisfaction.

"*He made his living
selling chopped up pigs.
He bought them from
his brother's slaughterhouse.
At Chinese New Year
he bought hundreds of chickens.
He slit their throats.
He plucked out all their feathers!*

*As he lay dying,
he pulled out
the hairs on his head
and the hairs on his body.*"

Nine old ladies nodded
their satisfaction.

*Preta: *hungry ghost.*

LOTUS POND MARKET

Looking neither left nor right,
a proud and sensitive Chinese face,
here by the Lotus Pond Market,
seems a little out of place.
Straight back, head held high,
adjusts her hair with manicured hand;
red panung, blue-and-white print shirt,
manouvres with care her sandalled feet,
as though she has stepped down from a higher band
into the squalor and dirt
of Chumporn Street.
But, as she passes the open shop,
something makes her stop
and look up where
she sees the fat Chinese,
above the street, at her table there.

The Chinese gestures, the girl hesitates,
thinks to walk on, stands and waits;
then steps up with an embarrassed smile
and sits down in the other chair.
The Chinese gives her a deck of cards,
talking all the while,
which the girl shuffles with surprising skill
and hands them back.
Without looking, the Chinese cuts the pack
and deals them professionally,
mostly to herself, occasionally
one or two to the girl, who looks carefully
at the cards she collects.
The Chinese gathers up her hand,
fans them face down
and invites the girl to select.
Hesitating, she takes two
and adds them to her own.
She watches the Chinese who
touches the girl's cards, talking in a monotone
suddenly broken by a sharp question.
The girl raises her eyes in surprise
and starts to reply,
stops, looks down again
and pronounces one word.
Slowly, she begins to speak.
An eddy of excitement
spirals up and straightens her back.

She points to this card and that
and taps them with delight.
She slaps her knee.
She bangs the table.
She stamps her feet,
bounces up and down on her chair,
laughing and flushed.
The Chinese watches her
with a slowly flowering smile.
The girl chatters on
and, with a final slap,
puts her head back and laughs.
Then she counts out thirty baht
for the Chinese, scrapes her chair
and walks on down Chumporn Street,
looking neither left nor right.

POMERANIAN DOG

Fat, white, hairy, Pomeranian tyke
sits on red Suzuki motorbike;
paws on handlebars,
oblivious to passing cars,
next to Michael Jackson look-alike.
MJ's body, face, paws (or feet)
are covered and hide
from the afternoon heat.
No sign of life inside
until a glove, large and black,
strokes the Pomeranian's back.
In front of Michael Jackson,
a red sunshade backs on
to a stall selling
blue shirts proclaiming,
Long Live the King.

From a tree that no one knows
a continuous shower
of blossom snows.

"Trees these days suffer.
All around them concrete
traps the heat
and roasts their feet."

Nailed to the suffering tree
for all to see,
a sign glitters,
Sago stuffed with pig
and banana fritters.

BURMESE BLOSSOM

The Tree of Life is in flower;
clusters of yellow shower
golden petals
on bare roads
in seasonal abundance.

One hundred and twenty-one Burmese,
including fourteen children,
travelled east looking for work
in a locked air-tight container;
twelve square metres
of standing,
enduring
jolting pot-holed tracks
and double-backs.

When the ventilator failed,
they started screaming
and banging the walls.

At Ranong
the driver unlocked Freedom's door
and finding the death count fifty-four,
fled headlong.

Those who survived have been given
two months in prison
before being returned.

The faded petals
have been heaped
by the roadside
and burned.

TREE OF LIFE

Mauve chrysanthemums one day older,
air-conditioning five degrees colder.
Darkaline tables, woven mats unchanged,
human beings have all been rearranged.
Same overstuffed, green cushion covers,
new middle-aged couple playing at being lovers.

Termite staffs make pointed spikes
to guard us from the motorbikes
that rush past fretted gates, green canopies
and rounded, caged-in balconies.

The waitress still hides every smile
quite forty fathom deep
but lets one out, once in a while,
when she thinks the world's asleep.

The traveller in her *Secret* disguise
sits no longer at the table,
has taken her gold-green eyes
and camera mind
off the jungled electrical cable
and left us all behind.

MONSOON SEASON

Chieng Rai and the Burmese Borderlands,
refugees and social disorderlands,
Golden Triangle and random roadblocks,
tornadoes in Rangoon and seismic shocks,
institutional American robber barons,
kalashnikovs and ancient cannons,
a cave temple with one patient monk,
ambulant hill-tribe people, opium drunk,
a house in the mountains
with peacocks and fountains,
hot springs to lie in and a lake to swim in;
six dogs, one man, four women.

CARNIVORES

Yesterday the dogs were frantic,
alternately ferocious
and looking for somewhere to hide.
There were Ah Kah tribesmen
on the road outside;
with hollow, dragon bracelets,
a single grain of silver inside
which rattles and jogs
and which they call the heart;
with dreamland smiles
which flicker and fall apart.

(They also eat dogs).

BEAUTIFUL PEOPLE

Super-talented children
play on the eternal beach,
building castles and cities
and civilisations and worlds,
anything, everything they want;
and try to keep all and each
out of everyone else's reach.

Dancing around hand in hand,
they themselves are powdered sand.

The sun shines down
burning them brown.
The sea rolls in
ironing everything
smooth and flat and thin.

MANTRA BOY and MANTRA GIRL

Close your eyes. What do you find?

Bars of light.
Vertical.
Horizontal.
Imprisoning mind.
If get through,
my star can travel.

Young girl. What do you see?

Sometimes two same bodies
separate,
fine and coarse.
Fine float short distance,
disappear.
Coarse dull like wax.
Sometimes burst of bright light
leave wax body.

Where does it go?

Don't remember.
Don't take memory with me.

MIRROR

I shone a light
into the mirror of your mind,
there was no reflection
and my light disappeared.
No recognition
beyond the blank stare
there.

SOMPHORN SAELEE

Suitable Gift was born into the Lee clan.
After the birth of her older brother,
her mother was paralysed.
She could only move her head and arms,
but became pregnant again.

After Somphorn was born,
the midwife put roasted rice grains
in a cotton cloth and pressed it on
her mother's stomach.
The skin was burned off
and the solar plexus damaged.

Somphorn's father kept pigs
and Somphorn fed them.
Jai Hieng, her elder sister, brought her up.
When she married, she kept chickens
until the government had them all killed.

Facial surgery;
she didn't like her face.
Eyelid surgery;
she didn't like her Chinese eyes,
wanted double eyelid.

Now her son keeps geese.

She buys and hoards
gold and diamonds.
*"When I look at them
 or think of them
 it makes my heart happy."*

HIYA (ELDER BROTHER)

Git lives in a big house
with eleven rai of land
on the river bank.
Inherited.
Everyday walks
to the temple shop
many times and back again,
always late.
Helps at funerals
and Temple functions.
Worked for Jai Saw's husband.
Went to Chinese houses
to buy their pigs
and catch them,
take them to the slaughterhouse
and sell them.
One pig in one basket.

Nowadays they just throw them
body on body
in pickup cages,
dispensing with baskets
for environmental reasons.

LIVING WATERS

All drink from the same pond,
Pride is out of place
(there is no owner).
Humility is out of place
(it is inverted Pride).

Enough that drinkers drink freely
and do not erect fences facing.

Set out to fence in a small pond,
you end up in a small cage
(which has no owner).
Wet.

LUK NIMITTA

The new Uposatha Hall
at Koh Chan Temple
is not complete
until boundary stones
are buried at each corner
to define the sacred limits.

The faithful pay
for gold leaf to stick on these iron balls.
They pay
for sermons to listen to.
They pay
to be splashed with holy water.
Holy water looks like H_2O;
but mantra words
in Pali language
from the mouth of a qualified monk
have been stirred into it.

Every year there is an annual fayre.
This year two million baht was raised.

Loudspeakers blare out
a popular song
about the Wheel of Fortune
which batters the eardrums
into submission.

*"If you can stick gold leaf
on the foundation balls
of nine temples,
you will not go to hell."*

THE INDIVIDUAL

is not indivisible.
In Stalin's underground laboratory
(or torture chamber),
experiments by laboratory assistants
(or torturers)
demonstrate
that if you isolate
each man's individual horror
and apply the sustained pressure
of consciousness at its very centre,
the whole psyche disintegrates
and falls from Grace
and the loose aggregation of parts
which replace it
line up like iron filings
to the research assistants' magnet.

"Under the spreading chestnut tree
 under the spreading chestnut tree..."

"Yes," says one of Lenin's old comrades,
*"I confess. I did put broken glass
 into the workers' food."*

MULTIPLE

In Buddha's sunlit laboratory
(or Dhamma chamber),
experiments by laboratory assistants
(or monks)
demonstrate
that if you shine the light
of investigation
on form, feeling, perception,
thoughts and consciousness
and apply continuous mindfulness
at the very centre
of the rising and falling
of these phenomena,
all things are seen
to be without a permanent self
and a state of Peace
is found behind the suffering,
which fevers this loose aggregation of parts
we claim as our own self,
and replaces it.

"We rise on stepping stones
 of our dead selves
 to higher things."

"It is excellent, good Gautama,"
says Prince Abhaya.
*"It is as if one might set upright
 what had been upset,
 or might reveal
 what had been covered
 or show the way
 to one who had gone astray
 or bring an oil lamp into the darkness
 so that one with vision might see..."*

ADVANCED TRAFFIC SYSTEMS

The oak stands firm and proud
like a mothballed British Lion,
Churchillian.
The snow piles up on those biceps
until they break and amputate.

The ash is altogether more lithe
and reptilian.
It resists the snow
as long as self-respect
requires, before yielding
and allowing the ice to continue
its gravitational slide
and test its weight against the earth.
Then it stretches out its arms again
to demonstrate the supremacy
of vegetable jujitsu.

The Siamese receive the latest batch
of pharmaceuticals from the west,
anti-pollution pills and environmental panaceas.
It is fair that those who exported the diseases,
internal combustion engines,
logging, factories and concrete, burning roads,
should, a little later, send the cures.

To conform to the requirements
of pollution control,
sensible speed limits
have been decreed nationwide;
twenty, thirty, forty, eighty miles an hour
to curb the drivers' actual speeds
of sixty, eighty, ninety and one twenty plus
(very plus indeed in this land
of paper begging cups
and red and black Ferraris).
The limits are imposed
across the whole network of highways,
dual carriageways
and one-way streets.
 "One way" streets are nominal.
Motorbikes always
and cars when they find it convenient
travel both ways at will.
The dual carriageways reverberate

with the growl of motor bikes
and cars speeding
towards you on the hard shoulder
and in the slow lane;
and cars which choose not to cross
the central reservation
and race towards you
in the fast lane.

Now everyone is happy.
With justifiable pride the Siamese
point to the environmentally friendly
traffic curbs and carry on
driving as fast as they can,
in whichever direction they wish.
The plague of motorcyclists
slide in and out like shoals of poisonous fish
in every possible direction,
carrying their female passengers
side-saddle behind them.
The police are happy
(important in a country
with semi-invisible martial law).
When the police captain
sends out his battalion
of armed subordinates
to collect a predetermined sum
by way of fines,
they find themselves like anglers
who have been given the keys
to the gates of the fish farm.
The roads are teeming with motorists,
all of whom are breaking one law or another.
In no time at all, assisted by
the judicious use of traffic cones
and waving of pistols,
the police have exceeded their target
and are back in their station,
sipping iced coffee and amphetamines.
The money has been counted
and the required birthday present
is on its way
to the District Police Colonel.

ENTREPRENEUR

The grey road to Chieng Sæn;
to the left
a narrow cone of red earth
rises forty feet
above the flat landscape
like a lingam.
A tall tree grows out
of its flat top.

Extraordinary.

Someone
has sold a hill
of rich red earth
down to road level
and left his signature
on this symbol of fertility.

CHAO TI

In the campus compound
of Klong Six University, Rangsit,
the students are practicing for Speech Day.
They stand in lines,
march up and down
and play musical instruments.
Porn's daughter is the Drum Major.
She throws her baton at the sky,
(which throws it back again).
Yesterday she fainted.
When she came round,
she said she had seen the Chao Ti. *
He complained that the stamping of feet
was disturbing him.
They took her to hospital
and she was unconscious
for a night and a day.
The senior students lit joss sticks
and knelt on the ground
to apologise to Chao Ti.
After that, Porn's daughter woke up
and was taken home.

Now she is unconscious again
and no-one knows what will happen.

* Chao Ti: *Guardian Spirit (literally "Lord") of a piece of land.*

LIGHTING CANDLES

"If I make merit by doing good
and share it with others,
how much will I be left with?"

"All of it."

"How can that be?
If I have a hundred baht
and share it with you,
how much will I have?"

"Fifty."

"How so?"

*"Merit is not money.
It is Light.
If you light a candle
and share your light
with your friends
by lighting their candles,
you have no less light;
but the room itself becomes brighter.
So it is with merit.
The world becomes brighter."*

ANOTHER DAY

AM
A scorpion in the bathroom.
A bolt of lightning
explodes above the roof
just as my hand
is touching
the brass and iron fan;
A sharp buzzing
in my fingers!

PM
Cataclysmic storm.
Lightning rushes up and down the mountains,
thunder shakes the roof of the car.
A deluge of hissing water
floods the valleys.
It may never end...
It always ends.
Everything does.

At the petrol station
a small crowd are huddled together,
pointing behind the shop.
"What happened?"
"A man has just been struck by lightning."
"Is he alright?"
"Yes, he's alright.
 He's dead."

YAKKHA

Chai Seng's mother
wanted a baby.
She prayed to the Yakkhas
that guard the gates
at the Temple of the Emerald Buddha.

Her daughter was born
with canine teeth
pointing up
into her lips
like a Yakkha's.

She married.
Her husband insisted
on a visit to the dentist.
Five teeth were replaced
to give her a human mouth.
But her lips still curl upwards
in a Yakkha's smile
and her eyes slide like lizards.

Her balcony looks over
the Burmese Highlands,
with their hill tribes and opium,
creeping mists and illegal fires,
flame of the forest,
Birdwing butterflies
and agonised cries of peacocks.

In a corner of the room,
a Chinese rosewood cabinet
displays some of the spoils trawled
in travels across three continents;
Chinese shoes to encase
the mutilated feet
of their crippled women,
who had nowhere to stay
and could not run away;
opium weights and guardian lions,
bronze protective leopards
presented to a French doctor
by a grateful Senegalese village;
antique silver beads,
Nepalese pendants set with topaz;
stone-age axe heads,

half-polished crystals,
opium phials and ostrich eggs;
art deco powder compacts,
a missionary doctor's boxed hypodermic,
a statuette of Vishnu from Ayudhaya,
incense burners and dolls,
a four–piece metal betel nut set
shaped like large pepper pots,
silver birdcage hairpins...

Early every morning
she gathers wild mushrooms.

She has six dogs
and her husband
has left a rifle
in her bedroom.

CHINESE WHISPERS

She sits in her room
with one hundred and eight
wooden beads
strung on a thread.
Every time she says *"Buddho"*
she moves another bead.

When Luang Por came to Bangkok,
her father took his family to
Soi Sailom to meet him.
*"It is difficult to meet an Arahat
 these days. You should ask for a boon"*
She could not think
of anything to ask him.
Luang Por said,
"This family is shining!"

Now she is sixty-seven,
married to a retired general,
who eats and sleeps.

"Buddho."
she moves another bead.

PIMSAI IN CAELO

"I worry about Siam.
I worry about Muang Thai.
Siam was ours,
Muang Thai we shared."

*"I worry, too.
I shut my eyes
to open the eyes of others
to what my people brought;
a certain agnosticism of thought,
a carefully defined democracy,
new cars, logging and pollution."*

"We did not support the Temple
but lived in our traditional houses
with sloping roofs
like dolls in a museum."

*"We brought new problems
for which we did not bring
new solutions."*

"I worry about my family.
We climbed Mount Meru,
passing the suffering of many.
When we look back down
we see the sufferings of all."

*"I am a caterpillar.
I clasp
yesterday's leaf.
I let go of yesterday's certainties
and reach out to grasp
tomorrow's transparent belief."*

"I am a frog.
I look up at the sky
from the bottom
of a well
and worry."

"I worry, too."

TREE OF HEAVEN

The Prince's palace,
in Pra Muan road, slumbers
behind closed shutters
in its small tropical garden.
Around it have grown a car park,
a dog pen of whippets,
a stable of offices, a restaurant;
a French-style café with darkaline tables,
where middle-aged women
meet each other and unleash
their middle-class children
on long suffering guests;
a shop selling organic vegetables
from the King's Project Garden
and whole-wheat French bread.

Along its inside wall,
a northeastern girl
sells pomelos and durian
mangosteens and rambutans.

The Prince is eighty-six
and slumbers, too, dreaming
of Dulwich and Trinity.
His public school education
featured being beaten with a slipper
despite his royal birth;
as a fag, he had been slow
to open a door for a prefect.

As a senior, he smuggled in beers
to share with his peers
and got drunk.
He was called in by his Housemaster.
"If you're going to drink,
 be sure to have a glass of milk first!"

He decided to smoke a pipe
as his father had done.
He climbed up into the bell tower
and puffed away in the dark for half an hour.
It made him giddy and he had trouble
getting down the ladder.
He was called in by his Housemaster.
"If you're going to smoke, avoid mild tobacco.

It will make your tongue crack."

Before leaving for England at fifteen,
he went to the shrine room
of the Emerald Buddha Temple
and, like every other Royal,
vowed not to renounce
the Buddhist religion.
To his oath he has been loyal.
But alien tides have flowed in
and lapped against his walls.
Across the road from the Tree of Heaven
is the Assumption Convent School
and to the left the Bangkok Christian College.

This morning the roads around
are jammed with cars bringing
a new generation of Siamese children,
in blue and white uniforms, in search
of a different sort of education.
They learn the English language,
that passport to economic success,
in exchange for the easy platitudes
of post-modernist Christianity
(and a substantial fee).

HORS D'OEUVRES

Jean Pierre had travelled in the Congo
before Independence destroyed
the last vestige of rural freedom.
"I came to a village and saw,
some bones on a pile of rubbish.
Child or small ape? I was not sure."

"Not long ago," said a villager,
"a pigmy came out of the forest
and went from village to village
looking for work. And yet
no-one would hire him.
What useful work could one get
from someone so small?
He was very thin. We offered to feed
him for six months and then eat him.
Because he was starving, he agreed.
We gave him the best food,
asking him what he thought was good.
We gave him girls for his pleasure.
He became plump and healthy.
He was happy. Everyone liked him.
After six months we killed him,
had a great feast and ate him.
The girls came too.
How can we ever forget him?"

HILL TOP SHRINE

Here, Chao Mère Sammukh
threw herself onto the rocks below
to escape from an importunate lover.
She has many followers
among the dolphins and sea people.
Even the Prince,
when sailing round Bangsaen Hill,
surreptitiously asks her
for a Bon Voyage.
(His crewman does not speak French.)

ANGSILA

Here the expanding world
has planted high rise hotels,
bars, bargirls and tourists.

Formerly they sold stone mortars
and Shanghai jars.

Young men hammered
thick bamboos into the seabed.
After a few months
they were covered by mussels.
The men dived and sawed
through the bottom of the posts.
At the end of the day
they were exhausted
and lay on the beach,
drinking mekhong whisky
and smoking opium.

There was a wooden brothel
with windows of long narrow slats
which opened vertically,
swivelling on central pinions.
When you walked past at night,
they slowly opened,
revealing expanding bars of golden light.
If you kept on walking,
they slowly closed behind you,
the pillars of light narrowing
to luminous threads
which disappeared into the silence.

PLUS ÇA CHANGE...

When peace breaks out, war heroes
take off their uniforms, sit in offices
and think up slogans to sell more petrol.
The Prince sat in the Shell Petroleum Company.
So he wrote:

Be super man
Drive super car
Go super sweetly
With Super Shell
SUPER SHELL! SUPER SHELL!
SOOOPER SHELL!

He attached a catchy jingle
and it was heard on the radio
and sung on the streets.
Did it cause cars
to avoid stations selling Esso?
It may be so. It may be not so.

When the Thais discovered synthetic fibres
(Look! No need iron!),
their cotton industry disappeared.
Tourists have been seeking
fruitlessly for real cotton.
As Peace stays broken out, other heroes,
with no uniforms to take off,
think up slogans to sell more shirts.
They write:
100 percent cotton.

"Why do you do that?"
"Customer want. Make happy."
"But it's not true!"
"Never mind. Never mind.
 No need iron! He more happy!"

Other customers are more happy too.
Vegetables have been grown,
with all the advantages of inorganic
modern chemicals, and shown
by American super salesmen
to be not only bigger and heavier
but kill beetles as well.
SUPER SELL! SUPER SELL!

Super salesmen
can also appease the hunger
of those who crave a green mantra;
Or-GAN-ic! Or-GAN-ic! OooorGANic!

"Cross-product Communication,
a policy of continuous development",
as taught by American super gurus,
means that your shirt, besides being
No need iron,
can also be
100 percent organic cotton.
SUPER SHIRT! SUPER SHIRT!

It doesn't even need to be green.

......PLUS C'EST LA MÊME CHOSE.

CITATIONS

Sariputta: *"There is nothing
which, when given up,
is not in accordance with the Path."*

I have wandered the orchards
collecting bunches of ripe lamyai.
I can rarely remember from which tree,
let alone from which branch, they come
but the taste is invariably
unsurpassable.

BLUE FUNNEL LINE

Passengers in a great liner
should be wary of jumping
into the skiffs and fishing boats
gathering round its stern
in order to feed off its excess
and the passengers' small change.

Upsetting and inconveniencing
small vessels entails a hefty penalty
(and you cannot easily
climb up again).

TONG DEE

Why are you lying down?
Are you ill?

No.
Just letting
bones settle.

Are you praying?

No.
Was rubbing
hands together.
Got stuck.

What are you doing?

Swinging foot
to find splinter.

Why are you scratching?

Not scratching!
Counting hairs.

How far have you got?

Lost count.

Can't remember
how it will be
yesterday.
Even if rain all day,
foot not go out,
head not wet.

Are all the mangoes the same, Tong Dee?

Yes. Especially top one.

MERRY GO ROUND

The Army stages a coup and replaces
the democratically-elected Government
which has brought economic prosperity.
(The Army wants a bigger share of the prosperity.)

The economy declines,
the paper Generals get richer.
(The poor get poorer.)

To get a bigger share of a new solution,
the Coup Leader creates a new constitution
and announces new elections.
To protect the people
from making wrong selections,
he bans, from the very start,
the democratically-elected Government
from taking part.
Despite his caution,
when the votes are counted,
the old Government, under a new name,
ends up with the largest portion.

The Opposition, which is still the same,
seeing they did not get in,
object and claim the elections were unfair
(because they did not win).
They organise street demonstrations
with martial coordination
and offer come who may
free food, a free tee-shirt and 500 baht a day.
Lest the authorities should eject them,
the army puts barbed wire
around the demonstrators
to protect them.

The Army's Chief Paper General
tells the democratically-elected Government
he does not want to use force to prevent
demonstrators causing chaos
and paralysing the city.
The Chief of Police General
shares his compassion.

The demonstrators ask the Army
to stage another coup and remove

the democratically-elected Government.

The Economy continues to decline,
the poor think it unfair.
The generals do not mind
so long as they get a bigger share.

THAI YAI

try to make their women beautiful
by putting brass rings
around their necks
to lengthen them.
The weight
bears down and displaces
their collar bones,
so their necks appear to elevate.

It is a branch of creative aesthetics
which has its equivalent
among the Benin in Africa
and in the mutilated women's feet
of Imperial China.

It does not make the women
more beautiful
but it does draw tourists
(as do Tracey Emmin's knickers).

DUSIT ZOO

Part of the Royal Dusit Garden Palace,
where Chulalongkorn built himself
a great golden teak palace
with the cutting edge technology of 1900,
was a private botanical garden,
full of rare plants and lakes.

In 1938 the Revolutionary Government
metamorphosed it
into Municipal Zoological Gardens
with animals and paddleboats.
In an enclosure of rock and grass
and paddling pools,
the two tigers can circumambulate
their world in forty five seconds.
They are fat.
They walk to get an appetite.
They eat only to sleep.
We look into their tiny freedom
through the bars of our great cage,
feel brave and shout encouragement in Thai
(they are Bengal Tigers)
and try to stare them in the eye.
They refuse to stare back at us
(they cannot reach us with claws and teeth)
nor do they stare at each other
(they have acquired the virtue
of mutual toleration in their tiny freedom
which we have not yet found in our vast cage).
To please the cameras,
one strolls down
from its ten foot high mountain
to the twelve foot long lake near our bars.
Turning its back on us,
it reverses to the edge of the lake
and tests the water
first with one foot, then the other.
Satisfied, it backs into the lake
until only its lower half is immersed
and reclines, head-high and proud,
staring away from us into the vastness
of its primeval inner jungle.

Tyger, tyger, burning bright,
in your forest of your night.

FREEDOM

Freedom from the Past
is the Present.
Freedom from the Future
is the Present.

The Present
is a crack that runs
through the universe.
Into it everything disappears
like snowflakes
into a bonfire.

For Māra's people,
the Present
is a mental space
filled with memories,
thoughts of the Future,
sense impressions
and a random stream of thought.

In the gap between thoughts,
the real Present can be seen
like the sun at noon
through dusty cobwebs
blazing in a clear sky.
(Or slept through.)

MÈRE SALEE

Flaws upon her face;
each indicates a place
where pain and sorrow grew
when a ripple of death-in-life flowed through.

Monitor her mind
that scatters the leaves the wind destroyed.
Monitor her mind
that blows its dead selves through the Void.

Each imperfection
is a recollection
of where unguarded thoughts have left their mark,
a clear reflection
(in a dusty mirror)
of a deep but dazzling dark.

GAOLER'S KEYS

A poem
opens a window
in the prison wall.

If it's not a poem,
it's just a picture
on the wall.

Who paints pictures
on the prison wall
is surely in the gaoler's pay.

May all beings be happy!
May they be free from ill will!
May they be free from enmity!
May they be well and happy all the time!

When friendliness puts in an appearance,
its starting place is non-interference.
Let the uncaged linnet sing.
Leave the butterfly on its wing.

When friendliness puts in an appearance,
Māra grasps its outward form
and wears it as his own disguise
with which he can his tricks perform.

He chooses it to make him friends.
He uses it to blind their eyes
and so accomplishes his ends.

He puts out bait for fish to find.
He leaves a snare to catch him birds,
sows seeds of craving in the mind
and mixes poison with his words
and all the whiles,
he threats and smiles.

Beware the Smyler with his Knife*
who wants your money *and* your life!

*Chaucer: *The smyler with the knife under his cloke.*

ASHRAM MELODY

The best way of enough is all gone,
for that there is no argument upon.

While there is still something in the dish
there is, in Mind, propensity to wish.

Wishing is a film that spreads itself like jam
and turns the dullest pebble to a fragment of "I AM".

THE CIRCLE LINE

Round and round the Circle Line
in endless pursuit of me and mine.
Familiar scenes go hurtling past,
each new vision much like the last;
grief and suffering, hate and pain
coming round and round again.

Where are the stops where the doors slide back
and offer a respite from a circular track?
Would I exit if I could?
Is there any choice but "should"?
When the stations slide into view,
is there a way out for me? And you?

The train slows down and signs appear,
once more decision time is near.

CONCENTRATION puts an end to endless travel.
MORALITY helps the karmic tangles unravel.
TRANSCENDENTAL VISION
unlocks the escape hatch from this prison!

KARMA

Karma runs its course
like some great fire
that burns towards extinction;
except that, all the while,
more fuel is added to the pile.

In the clearing up,
each has his share
or, like blue-necked Siva,
seeks to swallow
all the poison everywhere.

ONCE RETURNER

There in the dark, waiting,
is the Unborn,
looking for the opportunity
of moist earth
where it can seed and flower;
carried on the stream
of unfolding consciousness.
Only by constant vigilance,
is the tangleweed
of the Dreamtime
abandoned
to its stagnant backwater
of Time,
to return no more.

YAMA'S PAROLE

September Full moon,
the ghosts are released
to seek out their relatives
among the Living
who may make merit
to relieve their sentences.

Among a great many ladies
gathered on the balcony,
is one in a cream and grey wrap,
embroidered with pale blood-red flowers.

Mother, you are dead!

I know,
but it's not very nice
to be dead.
So I came back.

CHAKRI

The Lords of Life
are Tigers in their Wisdom.
They protect their cubs savagely
then cast them down from high places
to learn to struggle to survive.

To protect their fragile knowing who,
the cubs retreat into their wombs
and build palaces for going to,
which will one day be their tombs.

Coming back as Tigers,
their children forth they cast
to preserve (and lose connection)
with that fragile distant past.

APOSTLE OF TRUTH

The Thousand Petalled Lotus
in the brain is flooded with Light.
Diogenes,
in an off white robe,
still trudges around in broad daylight
with his lamp.

Have you found an honest man yet, Diogenes?

Only Myself.

DATTA

In the snow forests of Himavāna,
Lake Anodāta simmers like a jewel
among green-black trees,
slumbers in the scent of jasmine.
Its snow-born waters are deep-blue cool,
its silence deeper even than the snows
until gik-gak gik-gak gik-gak is heard
as Gunaras and Gunarees,
gold of skin, half-human and half-bird,
swoop down to their pleasaunce,
like wild geese to Solway Firth,
every return an almost brand-new birth.

Datta is dressed in white,
short black hair, no beard,
black eyes in Mongolian face.
As a man he lived among these trees,
now he has been the Guardian Deva
for over two hundred years.

JUNGLE GREEN

Trees calm the brain,
absorb the poison
of its thoughts
and return them
clean again.

Gong is the Land Guardian
of this place.
Old Chinese face,
Chinese hanging shorts,
pointed Chinese hat
of palm leaf and bamboo frame.
He sits with his back to the river
by the tumbledown remains
of his spirit house,
which has endured all of thirty years.

CONFUSCIUS HE SAY.......

You see them striding everywhere
from where there's here to somewhere there
with a box made of two shallow trays
which open out like a folding table,
like those in which a lepidopterist displays
dead butterflies each pinned down with its label.

The old Chinese has sat all day long
on that low wall in Surawong
with his box, staring intently
at the lottery tickets laid out neatly.
He takes a 1000 baht note from his pocket
and touches each ticket
stroking it thoroughly but gently.
Is he trying to magnetise them
to draw in a man who comes and (sometimes) buys them?

JEM

He shines out through his eyes his inner vision
of Syria, Damascus and abandoned churches
whose walls are incorporated into mosques.
His taste is for architectural researches
beneath the Present's outward-looking prison.

But now he struggles with the Family's Finances,
is chosen to establish checks and balances.
His Royal aunt, it seems, engages in unending,
and, possibly unintentional, overspending.

ECONOMIC CRISIS

BE SMILE DENTIST advertises down on
Soi Anuman Rajadhon.
Next door Anglo East Surety Broker
insures diamonds and gemstones.
Having struggled with the world's economic crisis,
faced with a shortage of government bailout schemes,
Anglo East has decided on a fundamental solution
and invited ninety-nine monks to come and chant
in this microcosm of pollution.

Here the open sewers allow scavenging rats
to escape the tooth and claw of ravening cats.
The one way street is choked
by two way traffic.
Pavements are blocked
by plastic chairs and tables,
charcoal stoves and washing bowls.
Food-sellers tap into the water mains
and empty refuse and dirty water down the drains,
adding to their universal smell
charcoal smoke, grilled fish, pork and chicken.
It is a jostling compost heap of life
serving everything from bankers to bacteria.

Last night the residents closed the street
and washed and scrubbed it.
In the early morning barriers were erected.
At one end an awning protected
ninety-nine white chairs.
At the other end, another awning covered
tables dressed with white and saffron
along three sides of a square.

Over five hundred people converged
and piled the tables high with offerings;
cooked and uncooked food, new robes,
bananas, sugar, coffee, cakes, tea,
tinned milk, incense, soap and pastry.

Ninety-nine monks filed in
and filled the chairs
with an early morning blaze
of brown and saffron robes.
The faithful knelt or squatted
on pavement and road

to receive the precepts of morality
and listen to the chanting.

By the power of the Buddha
may you all be happy.
By the power of the Dhamma
may you all be happy.
By the power of the Sangha
may you all be happy.......

The monks then filed towards the tables
and made a circuit
around the inside of the square,
while lay people filled their begging bowls
from the other side.
As fast as they were filled,
attendants emptied them
into the large black plastic bags waiting there.
Round and round they went
until at last the tables were completely bare.

The monks returned to their temples.
The people returned the street to the municipality,
rats, cats, bankers and bacteria.
The awnings, chairs and tables
went back to the hiring company.

The monks had received donations.
The people had made merit.
The owners of Anglo East Surety Brokers
had made ninety-nine merit.*
The demons of economic crisis
had been exorcised.

---

*Why ninety-nine monks? *There is a play on words here. In Thai the word kao "nine", with the same tone but a different spelling, means "a step forward" It therefore acts as an intensive. So if feeding one monk makes merit, feeding ninety-nine monks makes twice as much merit. No doubt if the road had been more than a back street, we would have seen 999 monks – even more merit and, perhaps, a serious and timely economic upturn.*

FOOTPRINTS ON THE MOON

Blue shorts, stained white shirt,
street market playground of dust and dirt.
Without the moral imperative of must
and the enforced need to understand,
he dances in a circle,
holding a yellowed bodhi leaf in each hand.
With all the self-assurance of thirty inches high,
he has no need to wonder how or when or why.

CHRISTMAS DAY ON SAMET ISLAND

begins in the half dark
with a six inch huntsman spider
exploring my chair,
ends with a Laotian girl,
with all the charm
of sibylline eyes,
wearing a fourteen inch centipede
as a writhing, living bracelet
that digs its claws into her slender arm.

In between,
courtesy of Thomas Edison,
there are Greensleeves, carols,
white Christmases,
and red-nosed reindeer
in different kinds of English
and Chinese fireworks.

ADESTE FIDELES

He stands opposite Uma Devi's Temple to beg.
He has a crutch, a bowl and one leg.
The other leg he lost in a motor cycle accident.
He has a pleasant face and every time we pass
we put something in his begging glass.

"You shouldn't encourage them," says Ray,
turning his face the other way.
"The Mafia brings them in the morning,
　collects them and their money in the evening.
　Even the children have amputations
　to excite pity for their mutilations."

Ray is one of the unhungry
who doesn't like to be asked for money
by the socially challenged. It makes him feel funny.
In Thailand he has to justify his uneasiness.
In England, where begging is against the law,
this feeling is easier to suppress.
The English view
is nothing new;
in Tudor England anyone, however poor,
found begging was flogged
"until his back was bloody"
both as a punishment and admonition.
If he persisted, he could be hanged in addition.

"These beggars are more useful than Chamlong."
The General's charismatic smile is a fixture
in Silom and Surawong
and threatens us from his picture.
"Beggars make it possible
　for us to give and them to live
　and we make merit as well."
"If Chamlong had to stand on one leg
　in the pollution of Silom Road and beg
　he would need oxygen."
A small, dark, Thammasat communist,
survivor of the massacres of the seventies,
with embryonic beard and matted hair, agrees
and offers his personal malediction,
"It was for people like Chamlong
　that the Romans invented crucifixion."

If Chairman Mao invented the Paper Tiger,

it was the Thais who invented the Paper General;
there are more generals than tanks in the Thai army.
But it was the British who invented the tank.
Their generals called them land ships
and they were crewed by sailors
until someone noticed that none of them sank.

    Rule Britannia!

JANUARY SECOND

The cars have fled the capital.
Taxi drivers have returned to their families.
The streets are swept and washed and clean.
The fruit sellers have gone back to their trees.

In Uma Devi's Temple
the air is thick with cataleptic incense
and jasmine garlands
and hypnotic with Sanskrit mantras
praising and invoking
Uma, Siva and Gnesh.

Here, as elsewhere,
as they get older,
people become more like they are.

MOB RULE SIAMESE STYLE

At the end of a year,
                        in which the army,
seeing that the people were being misled
into voting for the wrong candidates
and mistakenly electing
the wrong sort of parliament,
changed the constitution
to bring down the government
and banned the ruling party;
and the people voted again
for the wrong sort of people;
                        in which the army
protected anti-government
demonstrators when they occupied parliament
so that the Prime Minister's portly shape
had to squeeze through a window and escape
in a helicopter and take his government elsewhere;
                        in which the army
allowed demonstrators to occupy the nation's
international airports and bring them to a standstill,
so that those who wanted to arrive, couldn't get in
and those who wanted to leave, couldn't get out
and the tourist industry disappeared
and the hotels emptied
and the shops lost their customers;
                        in which the army
persuaded the Constitutional Court
to remove the Prime Minister
and ban the ruling party
since all the nation's problems had been their fault;
                            ...after all this, something new!
On the ninth of December,
mobs besieged Bangkok's Business Center
and brought it to a standstill,
so that those who wanted to buy couldn't buy
and those who wanted to sell couldn't sell,
in protest against a proposal to float Elephant Beer
(on the Stock Exchange not on the Chao Phya)
saying it would mean beer sales increasing
and more drink-driving.

These break-throughs (or downs)
have been masterminded,
and not a little funded,
by a blithe spirit who, when he was mayor,

displayed electioneering skills economical and rare.
(Are you listening, Hilary Clinton? Are you there?)
He is driven to a Bangkok street,
where he and the press have prearranged to meet.
He is photographed with a broom.
He gets back into his limousine,
is driven to another street
and photographed with another broom.
The smile does not change
but every street provides a different broom.
With his whistle-stop
(bristle-top) tour,
he sweeps away the economic gloom.

Some call it the *City of Angels*.
I call it the *Sorcerer's Apprentice*.

THE TREE OF MAN

The flowers of the Strangling Fig
are fertilised by wasps.
Its fruit is delightful
to green pigeons, hornbills, macaques,
barbets, gibbons and langurs
and ends up in their guts.
From there the seed
finds its way to a moist spot
on the canopy of a suitable tree.
It germinates and spreads down
a lattice of roots which reach the ground.
Once tethered there, it gives up feeding
on its unwilling host
and finds its food in the earth.
After many years it encloses
the tree like a shroud,
its crown overspreading
the top of its prey,
cutting off its light and killing it.
The support tree decomposes,
leaving a hollow, but structurally sound,
Strangling Fig.

In Europe, as academic
politocologists are well aware,
this ficus was first germinated
by Brother Marx
and became endemic
when cultivated
by Brothers Lenin and Stalin.

It has two natural enemies, capitalism
which attacks it with GM (jeanetic modification)
and, more recently, islamism,
a very effective non-specific homicide.

Recently a resistant Chinese hybrid
has been successfully introduced into Nepal,
politocologists now warn,
and is expected to replace nearly all
the existing native fauna.

NEANDERTHALS

Four men stand at a crossroads
on top of fifteen foot pillars
in the centre of the town
facing each other.
At first sight it seems to be
the ultimate western shootout;
no escape, winner takes all.
But it is not guns they are carrying.
It looks more like suitcases;
the ultimate airport nightmare,
no escape, no plane.
But it is not luggage they are carrying
but traffic lights which signal to each other
and control and direct
the smaller, weaker men beneath them.
For these are Neanderthals.

Two miles away by the side of the river
two giant karsts, shaped like the horns on a Viking,
rise up into the hot sky.
The limestone has been hollowed out into caves
and here Neanderthals had their settlement,
lived their lives and left their bones
for the Inheritors to find and wonder at,
to examine and reconstruct and carbon date,
to dogmatise and educate,
to decide an anthropoid found nearby
is a new type of primate, *
to transport tourists in fantail boats
and take their money,
to place statues on columns with stepped capitals
so that we smaller men in our cars
can know what we think they looked like.

So what *did* they look like?
They had short hair, designer beards
and a sense of decency
(like us they concealed their genitals).

Oh yes, and they carried traffic lights.

Siamopothecus Oceanus

THE ANCESTORS

Visible above mangrove swamps and jungle scrub,
accessible by boat,
these limestone karsts have been hollowed out
by the blind hand of rainwater
and the pounding fist of the sea
into multilayered chambers,
with pierced windows and doorways.
They are centred around a vaulted cathedral,
filled with artefacts shaped
without any art or skill,
no intentional shaping of the will.
They mimic the form
of freestanding natural figures,
column and image, bearded face and gothic demon.
This statuesque museum of limestone,
fossilized trees and rippling flowstone,
this vast cavern arched
with a stalactite studded roof,
has been landscaped and sculpted by Chaos.

The man is dark with black straight hair
that reaches to his shoulders.
His beard is short, his eyes are dark,
nose flat, jaw large, big teeth.
He comes, naked out of the water,
where our boat will later be beached,
carrying a fish, and clambers
up the cliff to the chamber.
Later, we will use rope and ladder.
The woman is almost as tall,
the boy stands three foot high
and is about seven years old.
Their language is grunts and gestures.
They are not afraid to see us move
into their present time
and look with mild interest
though we cannot communicate.
They meander and sit and sleep,
catch fish and small animals.
They have no fire and everything is eaten raw.
Their only natural enemies
are large grey snakes, which look like King Cobras,
for the big cats have not yet come.
Nor have the monkeys.
They have no tools but the rocks and stones

they can throw or beat.
In a smaller chamber there is one old man
with grey hair and a white beard to his waist.

They cannot see
the single Guardian Deva
whose name is Dāwa.
She has bare breasts
and golden hair.
She says she has been here
for a million years.

Her time passes,
she sinks back into the sea of Being.
She is now
a thirteen-year old schoolgirl
in Krabi.

Her successor is Dusit,
a giant with a club of fossilized tree,
fierce, with copper-coloured hair
and no beard.
When he was a man,
he cared for things and places.
He has been Guardian for
one hundred thousand years.

SURVIVORS AND INHERITORS

Caves, like palaces,
hotels, churches
(and shoes),
outlive their tenants.
Tigers came and filled the caves
with snarling and roaring.

After the atomic bomb fell on Hiroshima,
more than a hundred Japanese soldiers retreated here.
Most fell on their swords in accordance with custom,
grasping the hilts with both hands,
pulling and falling into an exploding sphere of pain.
The rest cut open their stomachs
and died more slowly, but just as surely.
Their flesh was eaten by tigers and dogs,
their bones mingled with those of prehistoric men
and the residue of earlier tiger feasts.
Thirty five years later, Buddhist monks came,
Japanese, Thai and Chinese,
and chanted mantras
for the salvation and reorientation
of the Japanese spirits,
who returned to Japan.
The earthly elements they left behind
were collected by the Japanese Embassy
(who also took the swords).
The caves were cleaned.
The tigers stopped coming.

Like deserted Indian Temples,
the caves were left to monkeys,
who jabbered and squabbled
with the sounds of enraged chickens.
Dun, as a boy, came here with his friends,
when they were bored with fishing,
to fight the monkeys for their territory.

Now the worn limestone caverns
are empty, silent, echoing,
teeming with images in parallel worlds,
waiting for the next arrivals.

Tonight one old monkey
sits motionless.

GETTING INTO HOT WATER

The forest is dense and undisturbed,
the trees high and overshading,
the birdsong harsh and shrill,
the giant cicadas persistent
like throbbing brass.

Paths have been cleared
and wooden bridges laid
over a latticework of hot yellow streams.
These infiltrate the vegetation
and send up clouds of steam.

They lead to waterfalls
where the water runs and jumps and spills
down through a series of pools
and shallow basins.
The water has smoothed and rounded the rock
and fossilized submerged roots.
The heat and minerals
prevent moss growing on the rocks
and they are unslippery underfoot.
Each pool is hot mineral bath and jacuzzi
in the middle of a jungle.
Birdwing butterflies glide through light and shadows
and skim the glittering waters.
There are no mosquitoes here.

GONG'S BIRTHDAY

Going out late in the evening
to buy sticky rice and bean curd,
down by the riverside market is heard
a persistent and continuous singing.
It is the Chinese invocation to Kuan Yin.*
Overnight an arena has appeared.
White-robed devotees kneel,
hold incense sticks and chant
before an altar offering a selection
of fruit to a life-sized collection
of carved Chinese monks.

What's happening?
It is Bun Tau Gong's** birthday anniversary.
Everyone is making merit for a week.

In this sea of white
are about a dozen initiates,
the men in red and blue halters
tied at the back,
the three women
in sumptuous, full length satin robes,
blue, yellow and pink.
All shake their heads from side to side
as though in a state of permanent denial.
With trembling limbs and unseeing eyes,
the men crack large whips, wave black banners
and wander among the crowd,
accompanied by white-clothed attendants.
Or they prostrate themselves before the altar.

These are mediums who offer
themselves as human vehicles
to the spirits of the Gong and his attendants
so that these can incarnate
for the benefit of human beings.
White-robed devotees carry blazing paper torches
with which they purify the arena
and sacred paraphernalia.
A large drum, two cymbals and a gong

  * Kuan Yin: *Chinese female bodhisattva of Compassion.*
** Tau Gong: *"Aged Grandfather" is what (some) Chinese call
   an old monk.*
   Bun: *His personal name.*

beat out a persistent rhythm
to which everyone moves.
There are two other altars
on which fruit is offered.
One is dedicated to Chao Ti,
the Lord of the land,
the other to the Deva
of the air above the land.

A living Grandfather,
dressed in a long red Dragon Robe,
pays his respects at each of these in turn.
He asks their protection and their permission
to perform today's ceremonies in their territory.
Endlessly shaking his head,
he peers at the auguries on the altar,
searching for evidence of the deities' consent.
Periodically, he strikes the rim
of a lacquered brass bowl
with a wooden pestle
and throws wooden shapes
into the air in pairs.
These are anxiously examined
and then discarded.
This continues until the desired throw
of these ritual dice has been obtained
and, we can assume,
permission gained
for the ceremonies to resume.

A red, wooden swinging ladder has been erected,
thirty feet high with eighteen rungs,
each of which is a steel blade,
cutting edge upwards.
By now each of the initiates
seems to have achieved
an acceptable convulsive trance.
The last to do so, a thin, intense young man,
has been sitting on his seat,
shaking and quaking
with determination for almost an hour.
An attendant shouts encouragement at him,
another whips the ground under his convulsive feet.
Finally he jumps into the air with a great howl
and rushes to the main altar.
Here he throws himself backwards
and is caught by an attendant as he falls.

They lay his motionless form
face downwards on the table
and remove his coloured halter.
All the male initiates are now bare-chested
and are led to the foot of the ladder where
each in turn draws an inverted S in the air
and mounts the sharp rungs barefoot.
The musical accompaniment swells
to a frenzy of supportive sound.
Two reach the top and shake their fists,
like goal scorers at Anfield.
One climbs up backwards
and down again the same way
to roars of appreciation.
The lady in blue scampers up light-footed,
then opens the front of her robe
and takes out narrow oblongs of paper
on which the initiates have painted Chinese characters.
These she throws into the air
and they float erratically down from on high
among the smoke and incense,
while excited devotees compete to seize them,
leaping up like trout after mayflies.

A red chair has been placed upon a table
and purified by fire.
A wooden cushion
with four-inch nails
pointing upwards,
is put upon the seat;
similar cushions
with similar nails
on the footrest,
the armrests
and the backrest.

From the Ladder,
the initiates are led to the Chair.
Seated, eyes flashing,
they bounce up and down,
trembling and rocking and shouting
until they are led away to exchange
their whips and banners
for swords with shining blades.

Then the self-mutilations begin;
the beating of backs with lighted jossticks,

the banging of heads on the ground,
the frenzied licking of blades,
cutting of tongues, arms and face.

Certainly there is enough blood
to excite the onlookers.
Undoubtedly the smoke and deafening music
assist our imaginations, though,
as flagellations go,
this one is not obsessive.
The convulsions and frenzy are impressive,
but the cutting of the flesh
seems sensibly restrained.

When I accompany the devotees
and watch them wash themselves
after their exertions and emotions on our behalf,
I am glad to see they have stopped shaking
and that their cuts are quite small.

Finally, lottery tickets are offered
to the Gong and his attendants,
those carved wooden forms
who have stared impassively
back at the shaking devotees
when they banged their heads
on the altar table and offered incense
to their lifeless forms.
Thus sanctioned and perfumed,
the lottery tickets are auctioned.

The things we humans do to tame
this mortal frame
and break the bonds
that bind us to it!

In the Ancient World,
which we admire,
respectable Thracian matrons would never tire
of stripping off at Full Moon
to chase wild animals
and tear them to pieces
with their bare hands.
Once, coming upon the poet Orpheus
and incensed, perhaps,
that in his isolation
after the death of Eurydice,

he had sought consolation
with satyrs and adolescent boys,
they tore him apart
and threw his mortal remains
(and his lyre) into the river Hebrus.

Tonight, at this Full Moon,
by this river,
I have watched devotions
generating high emotions,
while eating coconut ice cream
and savouring its flavour.
Yet never did the devotees in white seem
on the point of threatening me
with enthusiastic* Attic behaviour.

---

*Enthusiasm (Greek ἐνθουσιασμός): *originally meant possession by a god. In most ancient cultures, devotees and mediums went to great lengths to induce their god to enter their bodies. If this did not come naturally, they resorted to alcohol and drugs. In the case of mass enthusiasm among the Maenads in Thrace, the god was Dionysus. Here, it is the Gong and his attendants. In contemporary western culture, an obvious example can be seen in large rock festivals. Although, since "enthusiasm" has changed its meaning, this is often called "hysteria". But "hysteria" has also lost its original meaning. Certainly the enthusiasts at a rock festival are unlikely all to have wombs.*

THE BRIDGE TO PURITY

The next night is the last
of the Tau Gong's birthday celebrations.
It seems a pity to let it pass
without further observations
of these flowerings of the human spirit
and the extraordinary directions
the human imagination can give it.

A curved Chinese bridge has been erected,
the kind you see on Chinese porcelain.
To tone down the blank concrete terrain,
it is bordered with instant trees
and yellow banners hang among their leaves.
A bowl of fire protects it at each end.

For fifty baht up front you cross this bridge,
your name and date of birth
written on your receipt.
You are secure in the knowledge
that, if your sins are not too serious,
they will fall away from you as your feet
touch the bridge while you cross it.
But if they happen to be *very* onerous,
you fall unconscious.
It was not made clear to us
what happens in a case like this.
Certainly there was no mention of any surcharge,
nor any refund either.
(Nor was there any guarantee you were still alive.)

You don't have to be a believer to take part
nor dressed in white,
nor eat the vegan food that they provide,
(but you do need to have fifty baht).
It did not seem an excessive price to pay for
a clear bill of spiritual health.
Roman Catholic indulgences used to cost much more
and were moreover priced by item
(which is how the Vatican acquired all that wealth,
since there was no shortage
of sinners queuing up to buy them).
Islam, though just as willing to provide
hands-on spiritual assistance,
usually wants a limb or two up front (or from the side)
and does not encourage resistance.

As I was occupied in these reflections,
the coldest wind in living memory issued forth
blew up, broke out, in all directions,
but chiefly from the snows of China in the north.
This is a trying sort of wind to meet,
especially so close to the equator.
Even the bowls of fire could not compete,
spluttered laudably and expired.
Believers,
unbelievers
and middle-roaders
were all reduced to sneezing,
coughing,
sheltering,
wheezing
and agreeing
that it was freezing.

Everyone also agreed
that it was an *omen*.
But not of what.

Could I take the risk the deities of old
might have classed my sins as *onerous*
and intended me to die of cold?
And even if my sins *were* great,
they had not of late
been bothering me unduly.
I was pretty sure that they could wait
until I was a year older
and the weather a little less colder.
There seemed no need to go over there
and risk dying prematurely
on an imitation bridge linking nothing to nowhere.
So I passed up the chance to be spiritually well
and sought out the *warmth* of the Riverside Hotel.

It is universally agreed among religions
that these kinds of backsliding genuflections
when faced with physical adversity,
come high on the list of moral imperfections;
a clear indication of unsanctified conditions
which are found in most of us.
Decidedly onerous.
I obviously made the right decision.

PARALLEL LIVES

Sanor is walking by the river,
she is sixty eight.
Her face is beaming,
it is Uposatha Day.
She has been giving alms
at the Temple of the Jewel.

So many monks and hundreds of novices!

Her husband was a boatman.
He left the island of Phi Phi
just before the Tsunami
killed most of the boatmen
and destroyed all their boats.

Now he believes in karma,
making merit
and supporting the monks.

A man had cancer in the brain.
The doctor was about to operate
but the man died and as it was now late,
the body was left at the hospital in that state.
Ten hours later, the man came back again!
He said he had been taken to Yama
who told him it wasn't his time to be dead
and showed him Heaven and Hell instead.
Those in Heaven had done good deeds.
Those in Hell had done none.
Yama said since he had planted good seeds,
his cancer had completely gone.
He would not need an operation.
When the doctors looked inside,
they found it was the cancer that had died.

He said he had not really understood
cause and effect before,
but now he has seen the working of the Law,*
he spends his whole time doing good.

The monk said
everything happened
just like that.

*Law of Karma.

MUSHROOMS

From Western India to Tehran
the Litany is the same:

My Village against the World.
My Family against my Village.
Myself and my Brother against my Village.
Myself against my Brother!

KARMA

Vengeance is mine,
saith the Lord.
My tyres skid
on my blood
I spilt
on the road
I built.

BIG SNAKE

The Venerable Luang Pu Soh
is a famous teacher of meditation.
He is eighty-seven years old.

In the second year after his ordination,
while he was sitting in his kuti,
a large golden snake, six metres long
and as thick as a house post,
entered the hut, slithered straight towards him
and lifted him up so that he was seated on its coils.
It pushed its head into his body, but he felt no pain,
and seemed to push it out again
between his shoulder blades.
When he reached up carefully with his left hand,
he could feel its head above his own,
just as it is shown
in images of the Buddha.
After a while it crawled out and away
and he could feel his bottom touch the floor again.

In his sixth year, while walking in the Temple grounds,
he heard a loud voice inside him,
*"In your eighth year
your symbol will appear
through the air,
on the ninth waxing day
of the ninth lunar month.
He who has it now will come."*

When this day came,
he sat meditating as usual
in the early morning.
There was the loud rushing and roaring sound
of a great wind
which caused the branches of the trees around
to sway and beat against the ground
and a helicopter landed in front of the hut.
The pilot got out.
His clothes were green,
as was the cloth across his shoulders.
He had green armlets.
He had green skin
and carried a three-stringed violin.
The monk recognised him as Indra
and the violin as the instrument he had played

before the Buddha.
(Though he was not as beautifully arrayed
as in Temple paintings.)

Indra walked towards the kuti
and went straight underneath.

Twenty minutes later,
the monk climbed down
to look under the hut
but Indra was gone
and, when he looked, the helicopter had gone too.

After breakfast,
he was reflecting on this,
when a voice said, *"It's coming!"*

At eight o'clock, a white van arrived
and a couple got out, carrying something
wrapped in a white cloth
which they presented to the monk.
It was an image fifteen inches high
of Buddha seated on the coils of seven nāgas,
their seven heads arching protectively over his.
He named it *Venerable Father of Seven Kings*.

The image is famous and venerated throughout the country.
Copies of it and tear-drop amulets are widely sold.
From this image the monk has received
Dhamma instruction and practical advice
by means of an inner voice.
According to the voice, the image is eight hundred years old
and the voice entered it at its casting.

When asked, "Who are you?"
The voice will not particularise.

ONE-DAY DRY PIG

is for sale on the pavement
opposite Uma Devi's Temple.

A hundred year old shop house
is now all stripped wood and Georgian green.
On the balcony can be seen
plants and two vintage bicycles.
Hanging below it above the doors,
a garland of faded yellow jasmine flowers.

It is now a gallery on two floors
called *Kathmandu Photo Galleries,*
from which the daughter of a princess sells
avant-garde photographic facsimiles
of black and white erotica
and similar exotica,
posed in demotic metropolitan hells.

She is a devotee
of Rāmana Maharshi,
whose profound teaching
was to ask the visitors to Arunchala,
"Who are you?"

She supports urban
social unrest
in the manner of a princess
à la Françoise Sagan;

*"Comrade Sagan est venue en Ferrari,
bien sûr, apprécier la révolte
des camarades étudiants?"*

"Non! C'est faux: c'est une Maserati!"

EMERGENCY EXIT

I must be present now
before I can have a past;
I must be present now
to create a future then.

If I still my present mind
and exchange present thoughts
for nothing at all,
I have escaped past and future
and achieved a timeless peace
with no yesterday, no tomorrow.

I am
before
Abraham was.

TIGER CAVE TEMPLE

By the Temple Gate,
macaques lie in wait.
They squabble and fight,
like chickens, for the bananas
offered by northern Europeans.
They snatch
bags and cameras
and are happy to scratch
and bite
the hands that feed them.

An enormous limestone hill
three hundred metres high
towers above the temple.

A small staircase leads
up and over the rocks,
then down into the Khiriwong valley,
lush ancient lowland forest
with giant dicterocarps and fig trees,
their flared buttressed roots
offering comfortable back rests.
It is encircled on all sides
by steep overhanging cliffs.

The mountain is riddled with caves
which penetrate to its heart.
These are used by meditating monks.
There are also small wooden kutis
clinging to the rock face,
some of them too small to lie down in,
and cleared walkways.

Thirty years ago the Venerable Chamnean
came here to meditate.
A tiger walked into the cave,
but did not interfere with him.

Because of this, a temple was erected here
and Chamnean became its Abbot.
Now there are over three hundred monks
and nuns and also lay people collected here.
Chamnean is a famous Meditation Teacher
and his present cave
is a large modern building

in its own compound
with air-conditioning
and stainless steel decorative metal work.

The dell is unchanged, quiet and listening.
The macaques do not come here.
Outside one of the caves
someone has painted
in red letters *Snake Cave;*
and on an inside wall,
in faded white Thai script,
I am Buddha, in Pali.

We asked Chamnean whether
the story of the Tiger was true.
He said it was.

There is a Guardian Deva.

There are also washing machines in the dell.
And overhead lamps on the walkways as well.

THE DEVA

Sawang sits meditating
in front of the large Buddha image.
His loose top is gold,
his trousers gold and green.
He has short hair and a pleasant face.
He has been the Guardian deity
for five hundred years.
In the beginning there were many tigers.
The last tiger left nearly thirty years ago.
Now the nearest one
is five hundred kilometres to the south.
Is the story about the abbot and the tiger true?
Yes, but it wasn't a real tiger.
The deva took on the form of a tiger
to test the monk's state of mind.
Did he pass the test?
Yes.
Does he know this?
No.
Have you ever appeared to him again?
No.
To anyone else?
No.
Can you take on any form you wish?
Yes.
Can you appear as a tiger?
Suddenly there he is! Standing straight,
a fully grown, gold and black Bengal Tiger.
Can you appear as a monk?
A middle-aged monk replaces the tiger.
Can you appear as the Buddha?
No. The reply is immediate.
There are hundreds of monks here.
Are any of them Arya-puggala?*
Twenty.
Are any of them Arahats?
I don't know.
Is there still a snake in the snake cave?
Yes.
We look; a large black and yellow python
as thick as a man's thigh
in a hole in the back of the cave.

**The four classes of Noble Ones: the Stream Winner; the Once-returner; the Non-returner, the Holy One (Arahat).*

GRASS CUTTING

Today a hundred yards of green lawn
along the river promenade,
interspersed with small trees and bushes,
are ready for trimming.
Fifteen men and women
with strimmers, baskets and long-handled brushes
are given the job of creating great clouds
of fine green and brown dust,
interspersed with sitting and laughing
in a circle in the shade,
to give the heat of the day a chance to fade;
a not unpleasant communal occupation.
This would cause a sensation,
or even provoke outrage
in England, where one Council Worker
must do it all on the minimum wage.

LUANG PHO SOTHORN TEMPLE

The Buddha Image here is the most famous in all Thailand.
Despite the growing upsurge of factories
and industrial units, the economy of Chachoengsao
depends for its increasing prosperity
on the thousands of pilgrims who flock here
like seagulls to a fish factory
to be healed in mind and body
and have their prayers for winning lottery tickets
and the fertility of their wives granted.
(And spend their money on food, souvenirs and hotels).

This large plaster Buddha
has a twisted lip and hides
an older dark-bronze image
twelve inches high inside.
This does not have a twisted lip
and is of late Ayudhaya period,
with a high-pointed head-covering.
It is hidden to deter thieves
and guarded by five Devas.
Their chief, Sutee, has a moustache.
There is a more visible guard
of armed policemen.

The monk associated with this image
appears to have a body of light
without a sphere in the centre
and seems to be middle-aged.
He says his name is Sorn
and he died two hundred and forty years ago
during the destruction of Ayudhaya by the Burmese.
At the time of his death he was a Stream Enterer.
Now he says he is an Arahat
and appears here from Nibbāna
to promote Buddhism and help beings
cure their mental and physical suffering
by increasing their faith.*
And the winning lottery ticket?
He smiles.
If their previous karma is good enough,
they win it,
if not,
they don't.

*Just like Jesus: *Thy Faith has made thee whole.*

FAST LANE

In Uma Devi's celestial playground
in Moulding Lane,
the architecture bubbles upwards
in pastel plastic ganglions,
culminating in a pantheon
of opulent deities staring unsmiling into space.
At the entrance a stall sells you
African yellow marigold garlands,
a bunch of green bananas,
a bottle of oil, a coconut;
for fifty baht a tray.
You take it down the passageway,
past gilded animals and deities
and sellers of miniature (and not so miniature) idols,
until you come to the inner sanctum.
Here a hospitable sign tells you
DO NOT ENTER
and a Brahmin takes your tray,
dabs a blob of red
randomly on your forehead
and sends you blissfully on your way.
Your offerings are discreetly returned
to the stall that sells them
for economic(al) recycling.
If the secular world had learned
the secret of Uma's lesson
in husbandry and housekeeping,
we might have avoided this downward-spiralling
Great Recession.

GREAT SIVA NIGHT
proclaims the poster on the gate.
The Committee has chosen the date;
and, for the benefit of those seekers of bliss
who might not come through a whole night of this,
has divided it into three-hourly sessions, four in all.

Devotees are mortal,
gods (and goddesses), indefatigable.

ID CARD

The coloured poster on the bus shelter is specific;
the Cremation of the Great Teacher
will be held at the Temple of the Celestial Jewel.
Donations are invited for coffins, funerals
and scattering the ashes in the river.

In the middle of Chulalongkorn Hospital,
is a glass-walled air conditioned building
with a scattering of shoes outside the door.
At the desk inside, three smiling faces in a row
wait for more Great Teachers to appear
and occupy the vacant chairs.

I hand them a copy of my passport
and two photographs.

The conditions are reasonable.
I can be any age.
I must not have had any organs removed
or limbs cut off.
I must not die in a road accident
or from cancer.
I must not need an autopsy.
But I must get a death certificate
signed by a Registrar.

They will collect my body
within a radius of fifty kilometres
or I can bring it myself
within twenty-four hours.
If it is longer than this,
it must be kept in cold storage in a hospital.
But not in my fridge.
It must not be injected with formaldehyde.

While this is being explained,
the eldest smile is gently snipping away
at my photographs with her scissors.
With every snip, I can sense my life slipping away.
It is a comfortable feeling.
When they are the size of thumbnail images,
I sign the form and it goes
with the photos to her sister smiles.
While they are being processed,
she passes the time telling me

why her elder brother
prefers living in London to Bangkok.

At last I am given a card.
It has a small red cross on it.
It has my name and photograph
and is encapsulated in plastic.
It bears two signatures:
the Head of Body Parts Collection Department
and the Director General of the Hospital.
It is a Body Donation Card for Medical Study.
It is not transferable and I am number 11651.
It is not a credit card.

It entitles me to become
a Great Teacher when I die.
When I have nothing left to teach,
I will be given a free funeral.
I will be cremated
in The Temple of the Celestial Jewel
and my ashes will be scattered.

I must telephone the hospital as soon as I die
and I will need a Death Certificate.
This will help me prove that I am really dead.

I put it next to my driving license
and make a mental note
not to have a road accident
since this would invalidate me.

I step outside into the heat
and look for shoes
into which to put my feet.

A LA CARTE IN A JAI* FOOD SHOP

The Chinese soprano chants
an invocation to Kuan Yin,
the Compassionate One.

On the plate are pale yellow spheres,
the size of golf balls, split in two.
They taste bland, a little starchy.
They are decorated with fried dry chillies,
garnished with sweet and sour sauce
and browned on the outside.

There is what looks
like a blob of blood
in the centre.

What's this?

This?
The Chinese face
opens into a smile.
This is son-in-law's testicles.
Very popular!

---

*Jai: *Jai food is vegan food prepared by followers of a school of Chinese Buddhism centred on the Bodhisattva Kuan Yin, "the One who hears". She embodies Compassion and "hears" the suffering of living beings, thereby alleviating them.*

BAMBOO LEAVES

Their leaves of grass* emerge and fade;
with windblown rustling tongues converse.
The grove has grown throughout the universe,
spreads everywhere its pleasant living shade;
creating north south east and west
(the fierce, unending struggle to be best);
relentlessly growing.
The variety is unimaginable,
the sameness unknowing
and unknowable.

The grove is all its roots and culms and leaves,
yet every leaf contains the whole,
every living thing that breathes
and all its universes, as well.
All things are perfect
in their subatomic details
and reach out blindly to direct
networks of rhyzomes and roots
carrying new, all different, identical shoots
to every part of infinite space
until the chain of being fails.

And every leaf has a human face,
and every culm is a human heart.

At the end of a kalpa,
the grove gathers its energy
in an explosion of mass flowering;
an outward showering
of fruit and seed.
The clones wither and die,
the culms dry
and disintegrate
and crumble into food
to fulfill the eternal need
as a new regeneration germinates
and the whole grove reincarnates.

* Bamboos are part of the *Poaceae*, The Grass Family.

CONTENTS

BAMBOO LEAVES	9
POEMS	10
HOW IT WAS THEN	11
HOW IT ALSO WAS	16
HICKORY DICKORY DOCK	17
MEO	18
DYING RACES OF MANKIND	19
ULTRA MORES	22
JIT AND SUTIP	23
NOMADS	24
TALE OF A CHAIR	25
CITY OF ANGELS	28
JIEW	29
FULL MOON DAY THIRD LUNAR MONTH	30
SEE (GRACE)	34
BOEHM (BIG)	35
KWANCHAI (VICTORIOUS SPIRIT)	36
CHINESE NEW YEAR	37
MARTIAL LAW	38
JUSTICE	39
BURGLARIES	40
A FORK IN THE ROAD	41
SUPAPORN AT TWO A.M. *	42
NONGLAK (BEAUTIFUL WOMAN)	43
NOT ENOUGH, PLEASE	44
UNDER THE DARK OF THE VINE VERANDA	45
A CHINESE GIRL IN THE SEA AT SAMET	46
THE TEMPLE OF THE DAWN	47
THE NARAI	48
A QUIET WOMAN IS A PEARL IN AN OYSTER	49
AS A THING IS VIEWED, SO IT APPEARS	50
PUBLIC NOTICE	51
LEK (SMALL)	52
PHAK CHEE (CORIANDER)	53
NONG AND LEK	54
SOCIAL PROGRESS ON SILOM ROAD	55
STARTING OFF ON THE RIGHT FOOT	56
UMA DEVI AT HOME IN SILOM ROAD	57
"OH TO BE IN ENGLAND…"	59
SANGUAN (THE PRESERVER)	60
PAI DONG	61
THE HEART OF DARKNESS	63
"DOING THE SPIRIT OF GREAT SNAKE"	64
ORDINATION	68
NEW RECRUITS REPORT TO THE GUARDROOM	70

THE CLOISTER AND THE HEARTH	71
AWN (FLEXIBLE)	72
DEBTS AND TAXES	73
TWO TREES	74
LADIES FIRST (please)	75
KIK (RATTLER)	76
MĀRA	77
POETRY	78
MIDSUMMER DREAM	79
THE KING'S MINISTER	80
ALL DONE BY MIRRORS	81
AYUDHAYA PERIOD 17TH CENTURY ANON	82
THE MEDIUM	83
HUNGRY RIVERS	85
LUK CHANTANA	89
BODY SNATCHERS	91
FLOWERS OF THE HUMAN SPIRIT	92
THANK YOU MR. EDISON	93
TAOIST SAGE	95
SHE SAID...HE SAID...	96
VIPĀKHA KARMA	97
PHAK CHEE	98
NGU HAU BIN KEOW	99
ELEPHANTIASIS	100
JONG ANG	101
KINGDOM OF HEAVEN	103
SĀLĀ CHAROOSOMBHAT	104
AMPHAI (RADIANT)	107
PRATHEUNG AND THE MONKEY	108
THE PENDULUM	109
MÈRE RABIEB	111
UNDERTAKER	114
THE WAY	115
JUNGLE	116
DANCE OF THE SPIRITS	117
NEW YEAR'S DAY	122
YESTERDAY'S CHILDREN	123
SAMANASAKDI	124
REFRIGERATION BLUES	125
HAUT CUISINE	126
CANDLE IN THE VOID	127
WAT SUTAT	128
TAXI DANCE	130
WAT SRAKET	131
ĀMISAPŪJĀ	135
AFTERNOON NAP	136
BOA*	137

MĀRA'S SMILE	139
HIGH BLOOD PRESSURE	140
NURSE	141
DOCTOR	142
MAKHA PUJA	143
GOOD MASTER GOOD SERVANT	144
TEMPLE BEGGAR	146
JAI ING	147
NA-KHUN SPEAKS	148
LOTUS POND MARKET	149
POMERANIAN DOG	151
BURMESE BLOSSOM	152
TREE OF LIFE	153
MONSOON SEASON	154
CARNIVORES	155
BEAUTIFUL PEOPLE	156
MANTRA BOY and MANTRA GIRL	157
MIRROR	158
SOMPHORN SAELEE	159
HIYA (ELDER BROTHER)	160
LIVING WATERS	161
LUK NIMITTA	162
THE INDIVIDUAL	163
MULTIPLE	164
ADVANCED TRAFFIC SYSTEMS	165
ENTREPRENEUR	167
CHAO TI	168
LIGHTING CANDLES	169
ANOTHER DAY	170
YAKKHA	171
CHINESE WHISPERS	173
PIMSAI IN CAELO	174
TREE OF HEAVEN	175
HORS D'OEUVRES	177
HILL TOP SHRINE	178
ANGSILA	179
PLUS ÇA CHANGE...	180
CITATIONS	182
BLUE FUNNEL LINE	183
TONG DEE	184
MERRY GO ROUND	185
THAI YAI	187
DUSIT ZOO	188
FREEDOM	189
MÈRE SALEE	190
GAOLER'S KEYS	191
ASHRAM MELODY	192

THE CIRCLE LINE	193
KARMA	194
ONCE RETURNER	195
YAMA'S PAROLE	196
CHAKRI	197
APOSTLE OF TRUTH	198
DATTA	199
JUNGLE GREEN	200
CONFUSCIUS HE SAY.......	201
JEM	202
ECONOMIC CRISIS	203
FOOTPRINTS ON THE MOON	205
CHRISTMAS DAY ON SAMET ISLAND	206
ADESTE FIDELES	207
JANUARY SECOND	209
MOB RULE SIAMESE STYLE	210
THE TREE OF MAN	212
NEANDERTHALS	213
THE ANCESTORS	214
SURVIVORS AND INHERITORS	216
GETTING INTO HOT WATER	217
GONG'S BIRTHDAY	218
THE BRIDGE TO PURITY	223
PARALLEL LIVES	225
MUSHROOMS	226
KARMA	227
BIG SNAKE	228
ONE-DAY DRY PIG	230
EMERGENCY EXIT	231
TIGER CAVE TEMPLE	232
THE DEVA	234
GRASS CUTTING	235
LUANG PHO SOTHORN TEMPLE	236
FAST LANE	237
ID CARD	238
A LA CARTE IN A JAI* FOOD SHOP	240
BAMBOO LEAVES	241

Printed in Great Britain by
Amazon.co.uk, Ltd.,
Marston Gate.